# THE
# SOUTHERN
# RAILWAY
# 1923–1947

## STEAM ON THE
## PORTSMOUTH
## DIRECT LINE

### E.J. ROSE

ALAN SUTTON PUBLISHING LIMITED

First published in the United Kingdom in 1996
Alan Sutton Publishing Limited · Phoenix Mill · Far Thrupp · Stroud · Gloucestershire

British Library Cataloguing in Publication Data

A catalogue record for this book is available from the British Library.

ISBN 0-7509-1195-6

Typeset in Bembo 11/13pt.
Typesetting and origination by
Alan Sutton Publishing Limited.
Printed in Great Britain by
Butler & Tanner, Frome, Somerset.

# CONTENTS

# ACKNOWLEDGEMENTS

I am indebted to the following individuals and organizations for their help: Bill Bishop for photographs and information; J. Green; G.A. Pryer for track layouts; I.E. Robb; the late S.C. Townroe; the National Railway Museum, York; the Public Record Office, Kew; Portsmouth City Library; Surrey County Library.

I also wish to thank numerous staff of the Southern Railway and the Southern Region of British Railways for much useful information given to me during informal discussions, as well as in correspondence.

*Sources for Photographs*

For the loan of photographs I would like to acknowledge locomotive and General Photographs for nos 36–42, 47, 48, 50–65, 69–71, 74, 84–6; W. Bishop for 43, 49, 94; D.K. Jones for 66, 68; Surrey County Library for 5; F.E. Box Collection at the National Railway Museum, York, for 8–10, 14, 17, 22–5, 73, 87–9, 91, 92; Real Photographs Collection at the National Railway Museum, York, for 32–4, 46, 67, 72, 77, 78, 90; Lens of Sutton, Surrey, for 4, 11–13, 18, 19, 21, 26–9. The remaining photographs are the property of the author.

# PREFACE

The Portsmouth Direct line of the old London & South Western Railway, later the Southern Railway (Western Section) was always a favourite of mine. Living near it in Surrey for many years this was, I suppose, only to be expected. I travelled frequently on the line during the mid-twenties and early thirties, on some sections several times every week. From the late thirties until its absorption into British Railways on 1 January 1948 my journeys were infrequent.

Many older railwaymen have spoken to me in great detail about the line and of their happy memories of it. I have relied upon their experiences for much of the detail for the years 1946 and 1947.

The reminiscences cover the route from Woking to Portsmouth Harbour. The emphasis, however, is on Guildford with its big engine roundhouse, turntable, running shed, extensive goods yards, six busy platforms and a bay, and the bustle associated with traffic from seven separate routes. These routes were:

1. Waterloo main line.
2. Waterloo secondary (electric) line.
3. Portsmouth main line.
4. Reading cross-country line.
5. Redhill cross-country line.
6. Horsham branch line.
7. Farnham cross-country line.

The second route was the electric line via Guildford London Road and Effingham Junction which reached Guildford in 1925. Certain steam trains such as excursions, goods and van trains often used this route. The electric trains terminated at the bay formed at the end of No. 1 platform on the north-eastern side and provided a stopping service to Waterloo covering a large portion of the Surrey commuter area.

The site of the famous roundhouse engine shed, turntable and siding for the breakdown train is now a car park. People who knew Guildford over sixty years ago will remember the bridge over the railway which still carries the Guildford to Farnham road. Standing on this bridge, and looking down over the south side, the whole engine shed running complex was spread below. On the north side, a complete bird's eye view of all the platforms was obtained. It was really a paradise for the railway enthusiast. Now, the glamour, the interest, the incomparable smell of steam and hot oil wafting upwards, the whistling and the roar and rattle of non-stop steam trains speeding underneath has gone for ever.

It is particularly interesting and encouraging to note that every station opened from Woking to Portsmouth Harbour when the line was completed, is still open for passengers. One or two minor halts have come and gone and most intermediate station goods sidings are now car parks but not one station has been closed. At the end of 1947 all the goods sidings were still in use except those at Portsmouth (Greetham Street Goods) which were converted into an electric multiple unit berthing area in 1937.

The importance of the Portsmouth Direct line is in no doubt while Portsmouth remains a naval town and the Isle of Wight is still a popular holiday area. Moreover, large numbers of people commute from stations on the line, not only to London, but also to Portsmouth.

For steam enthusiasts, the extension of electrification from Woking through Guildford to Portsmouth Harbour on 4 July 1937 was the beginning of the end. Yet miraculously steam remained on the Portsmouth line to the end of the Southern Railway, though in a smaller degree. During the final 2½ years of the Southern Railway some lines which branched off the Portsmouth Direct line remained steam hauled entirely. These were:

1. Guildford to Reading.
2. Guildford to Redhill.
3. Guildford to Horsham.
4. Guildford to Farnham.
5. Petersfield to Midhurst.
6. Havant to Hayling Island.

Some steam continued in these areas up to July 1967.

A number of photographs have been taken on other lines or just outside the period covered by this book. There are three reasons for this. First, photographs of the Portsmouth Direct line between 1923 and 1947 are rare since it was not a line favoured by railway photographers. Secondly, wartime pictures were difficult to obtain, mainly because railway photography was banned. Finally, in order to convey to readers the atmosphere of railways fifty to sixty years ago or more, some pictures have been taken between Waterloo and Woking, at Charing Cross, Eastleigh, Strawberry Hill, Ashford, Reading, Westbury, New Cross Gate, Worting Junction, Bricklayers' Arms and Longhedge. This has enabled particular classes or actual engines referred to in the text to be shown.

What the future holds now that the wheel seems to have turned from nationalization to privatization is not entirely clear. I talked with many older railwaymen at all levels about the Portsmouth line. Most of them had spent a lifetime with the railways. They were proud of the Southern Railway and obviously dedicated to their jobs. One shunter, later a guard, described to me how he worked for nearly twenty years as a shunter. He assured me it was 'twenty years' slavery' but it was a man's job which he enjoyed because it was vital. What a splendid spirit and how right he was. Men like these made the railways what they were and it seems the general public took it all for granted. We all agreed that the end of steam was sad but that it was the inevitable finish of an era.

I hope this book may rekindle, in a small way, some pleasant memories for older readers and perhaps create for younger readers a clear picture of what railways were really like in those far-off days.

E.J.R., May 1996
Uplyme, East Devon

*Chapter One*

# INTRODUCTION AND HISTORY

The old London & Southampton Railway changed its name to the London & South Western Railway in 1839 but there was neither a complete direct line to Southampton nor to Portsmouth. Southampton was reached via Bishopstoke, now called Eastleigh, in 1840. In 1839, however, a branch line was built from Fareham to Gosport whereby travellers for Portsmouth used a ferry, or so-called Floating Bridge, from Gosport to Portsmouth. By 1847, the London Brighton & South Coast Railway reached Portsmouth Town station, now called Portsmouth & Southsea, but the journey from London Bridge station via Brighton, Chichester and Havant was 95 miles. It was a journey no quicker than that via Bishopstoke, Fareham and Gosport which totalled 87½ miles. In 1848 the LSWR built a branch from Fareham via Cosham to Port Creek Junction where it made a connection with the LBSCR line from Havant to Portsmouth Town station. This route covered 91½ miles if one travelled from the London terminus at Nine Elms via Basingstoke, Winchester, Eastleigh and Fareham to Portsmouth Town station. The direct line via Woking, Godalming, Haslemere and Havant, where it joined up with the LBSCR line, was completed in 1859. The section to Guildford was open in 1845, to Godalming in 1852, later used as Godalming Goods, and finally to Havant in 1859. The distance from Waterloo to Portsmouth Town was 74 miles and about 70 miles from Nine Elms. This was much shorter than the three earlier routes. The LBSCR actually shortened their route to London to 87 miles some years later travelling via Pulborough, Horsham and Dorking North.

Returning now to the direct Portsmouth line, there were three important additions to it later. In 1864 the Midhurst branch from Petersfield was opened. Next, in 1876, the extension line from Portsmouth Town to Portsmouth Harbour was completed. Finally there was the opening of Fratton station in 1885. While on the subject of the history at the Portsmouth end of the line, it is interesting to note that Portsmouth Town station was renamed Portsmouth & Southsea in 1861 but resumed its original name in 1876 only to revert back to its 1861 name in 1921, a name it has retained ever since.

The idea to extend the line from Guildford via Haslemere to Havant was planned as early as 1852 by the famous Victorian engineer Thomas Brassey. The extension received parliament's approval in 1853. The line was originally only single with passing loops as it was constructed as cheaply as possible. It had many sharp curves for a main line as well as stiff gradients and only two tunnels, at Buriton and Guildford. Not very long after completion, part of the Guildford tunnel fell in. The tunnel was then altered to two parts with a short cutting in between. It was not until 1876 that the line was doubled.

It has been reported that when the LSWR tried to run the first train from London to

Portsmouth via the direct route, the LBSCR blocked the line at Havant Junction and a pitched battle ensued with each company bringing up reinforcements. That was not strictly correct. The LBSCR did in fact block the line for the LSWR but then the unfortunate driver of a Brighton to Portsmouth train belonging to the LBSCR was manhandled by the LSWR supporters and taken off the footplate. The dispute was decided in the courts. In the meantime, the LSWR stopped their trains at a temporary station short of Havant where passengers for Portsmouth completed their journey by horse bus. The courts decided in favour of the LSWR. The LBSCR did consider appealing but finally favoured a fierce fares competition with their rival. This 'war' went on from March until August 1859 to the obvious advantage of the passengers. Finally the two companies came to a peaceful settlement and worked the line amicably until 1923 when they both became part of the Southern Railway. I am told that during the days of the Southern, Fratton shed was divided between the Western and Central sections, i.e. the two former companies' spheres of interest. This independent control lasted right to the end of the Southern Railway on 31 December 1947. Certainly, during Southern Railway days, South Western engines and passenger rolling stock kept to the old LSWR territory and Brighton locomotives and stock kept to their area.

Therefore, by 1859, there were three routes from London to Portsmouth open. Firstly, London, Woking, Guildford and Havant to Portsmouth at 74 miles; secondly, London, Brighton, Chichester and Havant at 95 miles; and finally, London, Woking, Basingstoke, Winchester, Bishopstoke, Fareham and Cosham at 94½ miles. The line from Havant to Port Creek Junction was owned by the LBSCR but the LSWR had running powers on it. From Fareham the LSWR extended their line via Cosham to Port Creek Junction. From Cosham to Portsmouth Town the line was jointly owned by the two companies as was the 1876 extension to Portsmouth Harbour.

This is only a brief summary of the history at the Portsmouth end of the line which readers will need as background. For a very detailed account covering the period from the early 1830s onwards, I would recommend a study of *The Portsmouth Papers No. 6 – Portsmouth Railways* by Edwin Course. The date of publication was 1969 but it was still available in 1985. Local papers and records in Portsmouth City Library also give much information.

On 1 January 1923, the Southern Railway was formed by an amalgamation of the LSWR, the LBSCR, the SE & CR (South Eastern & Chatham Railway), and a number of small railways including those in the Isle of Wight. The Portsmouth Direct line was the third most important main line of the LSWR. The West of England main line to Exeter and beyond was the most important followed by the Southampton, Bournemouth and Weymouth line. So far as the Portsmouth line was concerned, there was little immediate change after the grouping. Electrification of the Portsmouth line was discussed but it was neither imminent nor earmarked for introduction in the future.

The LSWR now became the Western Section of the SR. It was a railway which had been extremely well served by its Locomotive Superintendents, long since known as Chief Mechanical Engineers by the time the SR was formed. When the London & Southampton Railway became the LSWR in 1839, J. Woods was the incumbent Locomotive Superintendent. He was succeeded in turn by J.V. Gooch in 1841, Joseph

Beattie in 1850, his son William Beattie in 1871, William Adams in 1877, and Dugald Drummond in 1895. After Drummond's tragic death in 1913, Robert Urie was appointed. When the SR was formed in 1923, Richard Maunsell was appointed to the post having had a similar post with the South Eastern & Chatham Railway at Ashford, Kent. Maunsell remained as CME until 1937 when he was succeeded by Oliver Bulleid. Bulleid stayed on until after the end of the SR but he left British Railways in 1949.

From 1923 to 1947, locomotives designed by six of the CMEs mentioned were still doing yeoman service on the Southern Railway. Many of these engines lasted right to the end of steam on British Railways Southern Region in 1967. Examples of engines either now operating or under complete overhaul on privately owned lines at the time of writing are:

| | |
|---|---|
| Joseph Beattie | 2–4–0T, BR No. 30585, lately at Quainton Road. |
| William Adams | 4–4–2T, SR No. 3488, on the Bluebell Railway. |
| Dugald Drummond | T9 class 4–4–0, SR No. 120, in use on the Mid-Hants Railway. |
| Robert Urie | S15 class 4–6–0, SR No. 506, in use on the Mid-Hants Railway. |
| Richard Maunsell | Q class 0–6–0, SR No. 541, in use on the Bluebell Railway. |
| Oliver Bulleid | 'Merchant Navy' class 4–6–2, BR No. 35028 *Clan Line*, in use on British Rail for special trains. |

Several of Maunsell's engines survive in working order under private ownership. No. 850 *Lord Nelson* is perhaps best known and three of his famous 'Schools' class are in working order, namely Nos. 925 *Cheltenham*, 926 *Repton* and 928 *Stowe*. Also some of Maunsell's N and U Class 2–6–0s survive. All these engines testify to the soundness of his designs. Finally, No. 777 *Sir Lamiel*, the N15 class 'King Arthur' which is basically one of Urie's designs, is still among the restored engines. The Bulleid Pacifics were of course comparatively new and several are still in working order.

At this stage, I should perhaps explain that engines in the 'Lord Nelson' class were extremely rare visitors to the Portsmouth line, at least up to 1937. Apart from No. 861 *Lord Anson* to which I refer in Chapter Three. I have been able to trace only two other visits. These were in 1947 in connection with a Royal Train journey to and from Portsmouth. I have dealt with this in greater detail in the Epilogue.

In the late twenties the SR General Manager was Sir Herbert Walker KCB who was previously a London & South Western man. Astute and very capable, he did much to expand the public image of the Southern. He was behind the big publicity build-up and the formation of a public relations policy. All the principal Southern Railway officers were based at Waterloo except the Chief Commercial Manager who was at London Bridge. In 1923 and 1924 the widespread naming of engines was a new practice so far as the Southern was concerned. Although there were small numbers of engines bearing names on the Central Section, ex-London Brighton & South Coast Railway locomotives, this new policy did much to keep the Southern in the public eye. The seventy-four 'King Arthur' 4–6–0s were the first whole class to be named. These were followed by the sixteen 'Lord Nelson' 4–6–0s and the forty 'Schools' class 4–4–0s. At the end of 1931 only ten 'Schools' engines were in service, the remainder being built and in service by 1935. In that year ten of the 'Schools' class were allocated to Fratton shed for use on the Portsmouth Direct line.

I have given all the foregoing data which relates to the then newly formed Southern Railway as a background history but much of it is relevant to the Western Section in general and to the Portsmouth Direct line as well.

Southern train services were expanded and there was also a general speeding up of long-distance services from 1927. Competition from the long-distance motor coach which had developed from the old open motor charabanc was only just beginning in the mid-twenties. Long-distance lorry traffic existed, solid tyred lorries were only just being converted to pneumatic tyres, but the threat to the railways' long-distance goods and perishable traffic was no more than a faint cloud on the horizon. In any case, goods traffic was never a large proportion of total traffic on the Woking to Portsmouth line in steam days. The Southern as a whole was essentially a passenger carrying line and this was particularly so on the Western Section.

The Waterloo to Portsmouth and Woking to Portsmouth trains carried a large number of passengers and their luggage en route to the Isle of Wight during the summer. The destination boards on the faster trains starting from Waterloo carried the wording 'Waterloo, Portsmouth, Isle of Wight'. Through tickets to all stations on the Isle of Wight, there were over thirty stations on the island, were available from mainland stations and the fare on the steamer to Ryde from Portsmouth Harbour was of course included. Summer runabout tickets were available for unlimited travel on the island for a week at a mere 10s (50p) third class.

Another lucrative source of revenue on the Portsmouth Direct line was the movement of naval personnel en route to or from Portsmouth and Chatham via Waterloo, Victoria or Cannon Street stations, as well as from sailors going on leave or returning to their ships in Portsmouth.

In around 1928 or 1929 a number of small firms, and two fairly large companies, were expanding their motor coach services between Portsmouth and London. One large company even commenced a service between Chatham and Portsmouth, clearly with a view to attracting naval traffic. By 1932, no fewer than ten firms were operating between Portsmouth and London. Such was the competition beginning for the railway but even by the early thirties the train was faster, more comfortable and vastly more reliable. Then, as now, it was very much safer to travel by rail. The railway was nevertheless troubled by the cheap fares offered by the motor coach firms; in some cases about half the train fare. All their vehicles were petrol driven, for the diesel driven motor coach had not yet arrived. Some of these motor coaches were quite smooth and reasonably comfortable, others were distinctly grubby and uncomfortable. Interior heating was virtually non-existent and in winter this left much to be desired. Furthermore, a stop for refreshments halfway to or from London added at least another half an hour to the journey time which was in the region of 3 to 3½ hours. The schedule for the fast trains was 1 hour 40 minutes later reduced to 1½ hours. In practice, the summer expresses took a few minutes longer while on Saturdays most of the fast trains were allowed up to ten minutes extra for

1  A Leyland 'Tiger' 30-seater motor coach en route from Chatham to Portsmouth, about to leave Hindhead, Surrey, after a meal stop (1929)

2  A London-bound Dennis 18-seater motor coach comes to grief on the A3 near Hindhead (1931)

**3** Front view of a Reo 30-seater motor coach about to leave Hindhead for Portsmouth (1928)

the whole journey, due very largely to congestion between Havant and Portsmouth. There were several semi-fast trains which covered the journey in 2 to 2½ hours. All these trains were faster than the road motor coach. Compared with the 1914 London & South Western Railway timetable there had been a great improvement not only in speed but also in the frequency of trains. After 1935, the fast trains between Waterloo and Portsmouth worked to a 1½ hour schedule mainly to ensure their superiority over the motor coach which was showing a steady improvement in journey times. Even so, an average speed of between 22 and 25 mph from London to Portsmouth, including a refreshment stop, was the quickest achieved by motor coach in the mid-thirties, and fortunately for the railway this was still double the fastest train times. The 'Schools' class locomotives arrived on the scene in 1935 and this event marked a subsequent improvement in the train times.

On 4 July 1937, electric trains started on the public service from Waterloo to Portsmouth Harbour. However, steam continued on goods, van, excursion and cross-country trains. Steam also deputized for the odd failure of the electric train. Incredibly, steam lingered on the Portsmouth Direct line right up to the end of the Southern Railway on 31 December 1947. Even that was not the final end of steam for some cross-country and van trains were steam hauled right to the very end of steam in 1967. I also discovered in my researches that during the electrification of the Bournemouth line it was necessary to route some Bournemouth to Waterloo steam trains via Farlington Junction and Woking on the Portsmouth Direct line.

*Chapter Two*

# THE ROUTE FROM WATERLOO TO PORTSMOUTH HARBOUR

The new Waterloo terminus station with twenty-one platforms was officially opened by King George V in 1925 although it had been used all the time during alterations and additions. Portsmouth Direct line trains which started from Waterloo used the same route as the West of England, Southampton, Bournemouth and Weymouth trains as far as Woking Junction, 24¾ miles from Waterloo. The line to Portsmouth branches off at Woking Junction in a south-westerly direction, and this is the actual starting point of the line.

The Nine Elms to Woking section was the first part of the old London & Southampton Railway but the Waterloo to Nine Elms section was added by the London & South Western Railway later. The line to Southampton was laid out and constructed under the direction of Joseph Locke, one of the most capable of the Victorian civil engineers, and was completed in 1840.

Apart from the immediate exit from Waterloo, which is quite sharply curved, the line is reasonably straight after Vauxhall, 1¼ miles from Waterloo. From passing Clapham Junction, 4 miles, with its twenty-four platforms, a straight run takes the line to Wimbledon, 7¾ miles, and Raynes Park, 8¾ miles, where the line for Leatherhead diverges on the Down side. The line then continues to New Malden, 9¾ miles, Berrylands, 11 miles, and Surbiton, 12 miles. The last three stations have always had heavy commuter traffic. Next comes Hampton Court Junction, 13¼ miles, followed by Esher, 14¼ miles, with Sandown Park horse-racing track visible on the Down side of the line just after the station. After Hersham, 16 miles, it is virtually a straight run with a slightly rising gradient through Walton-on-Thames, 17¼ miles, and Weybridge, 19¼ miles. The average gradient from Waterloo to this point is 1 in 1,800. From here the line continues on a rising gradient of 1 in 240 taking the train past the old Brooklands motor racing track below the railway embankment on the Down side. Byfleet, 21¾ miles, is quite close to the Byfleet Banking of the old motor racing track. Still on a rising gradient Woking is reached after 24¼ miles. Half a mile further on the Portsmouth Direct line turns off on the Down side.

Notable features between Waterloo and Woking are the number of flying and burrowing junctions. These enable trains to leave or join the main line without affecting other trains using the fast lines and with minimum delay to trains on the slow lines. Both Southern Railway and later British Railways used the two inner lines as fast and the two outer lines as slow. On this four-track run from Waterloo, the line does not converge to double track until just west of Basingstoke at Worting Junction, 50¼ miles from Waterloo. There have, however, always been more than four running tracks as far as Clapham Junction.

The electric trains, which first reached Guildford from Waterloo in 1925, left the main line at Raynes Park or Hampton Court Junctions. They were the only electric trains using Guildford until the electrification of the Portsmouth Direct line in July 1937.

Waterloo steam trains for the Portsmouth line could be divided broadly into two categories as far as Woking. They were the express trains which ran non-stop to Portsmouth and the semi-fast trains calling either at Surbiton or Weybridge and Woking before joining the Portsmouth line. This pattern remained with few changes until full electrification in July 1937. The fast steam trains out of Waterloo, such as the 11.50 a.m., 1.50 p.m. and 3.50 p.m. passed through Woking in around 30 minutes and Guildford in 38 to 40 minutes, an average speed of 45 to 50 mph. Nowadays the fast or semi-fast electric trains are allowed 26 minutes to Woking and 35 to 39 minutes to Guildford, stopping at both places. To Guildford therefore, the electric trains average 46½ to 50 mph.

In the 50 mile run from Woking to Portsmouth Harbour there were 14 intermediate stations and two halts giving an average of one station or halt every 3⅛ miles. The greatest distance between stops was the 8¼ miles from Petersfield to Rowlands Castle. The shortest distance was the ¾ mile between Portsmouth & Southsea and Portsmouth Harbour stations.

The Portsmouth Direct is of double track from the junction at Woking all the way to Portsmouth Harbour. The layout at Woking and at Portsmouth Harbour has not changed basically in the past seventy years. There used to be an extensive goods yard at Woking together with carriage and engineers' sidings but only a small turntable and small engine shed at the Waterloo end of the station on the Down side.

From Woking, always a busy and important junction in steam days, four running lines passed through for the West of England stations in Cornwall, Devon, Somerset, Dorset, Hampshire and Surrey, as well as for Portsmouth and the Isle of Wight. The Portsmouth Direct line diverged to the left on the Down side exactly half a mile west of Woking station.

At 2¾ miles from Woking, Worplesdon station is reached after one mile on a gently falling gradient changing to a short rise of 1 in 110 into the station. As now, Worplesdon was mainly a Waterloo commuter station and, although there were some sidings, the bulk of the traffic consisted of commuters. A fairly straight run of some 3½ miles with a slight rise followed by a short falling gradient midway brings you to Guildford. This was the largest station between Waterloo and Portsmouth Harbour. In the late twenties and early thirties this was a very busy station indeed. Not only was there a heavy commuter traffic, but large quantities of coal, machinery, and general merchandise were handled at Guildford. On market days many wagon loads of cattle passed through the cattle sidings. The erstwhile Margate to Birkenhead trains, with through coaches to and from Portsmouth and Bournemouth to be detached or attached, stopped at Guildford. These trains of course used the Tonbridge–Redhill–Guildford–Reading General lines. The only other station on the line which also dealt with really long-distance trains comparable

4  The station at Woking after electrification, looking westwards

with the Margate to Birkenhead train was Portsmouth & Southsea. For example, there were trains from Portsmouth & Southsea to Liverpool, Manchester, Newcastle-on-Tyne, Bradford, Bristol, Cardiff, Plymouth, Brighton, Hastings, Glasgow and Edinburgh with numerous connections to other far-flung places. Whereas coaches were added or taken off at Guildford, at Portsmouth & Southsea, by contrast, Brighton and Hastings trains reversed but as a rule no coaches were added or taken off.

Like Woking, Guildford had a station pilot engine which was engaged mainly in carriage shunting during the day. For many years in the middle twenties, one of William Adams' outside cylinder 4–4–0s No. E595 of the X2 class fulfilled the station pilot duty. This engine was clearly awaiting a major overhaul but, nevertheless, was always in an immaculate condition externally with polished brasswork and gleaming green paint, a real joy to see.

Readers will see from the Guildford track layout in Appendix I that virtually the whole station, together with its associated tracks and sidings, was laid in straight lines within a vast rectangle. Moreover, this site was practically level which clearly facilitated train running and shunting operations in every way. The line to Reading was the only exception since it climbed away to the north-east on a 1 in 100 gradient. The engine running shed, turntable and siding berthing the breakdown crane and train were at the western end of the station on a slight curve, and somewhat cramped by surrounding high ground. In the mid-twenties, and thereafter, Guildford had seven through platforms and a bay platform. During the course of some local research I managed to obtain some very

**5** U class 2–6–0 No. 1621 leaving Guildford with a van train. Part of the roundhouse and turntable appear on the right. Although the picture was taken in 1937, the track layout was unchanged from 1917

early photographs of Guildford station in 1850 and 1872. Surprisingly, the layout of the first three platforms and the small carriage sidings west of Platform 1, now Platform 2, is virtually unchanged in 1995. In 1872, the station name board proclaimed 'Guildford Junction'.

The site of Guildford station must have been very carefully selected, for not only is it level and straight, but it is very conveniently situated close to the city centre. Guildford is broadly a place built up two sides of a flattened letter V, the River Wey flowing through the bottom of the V. The railway passes through one of the arms of the V almost at its lowest point. The only real obstacle the railway civil engineers met was St Catherine's Hill through which they had to tunnel at the western end of the station.

With numerous parallel running lines or loop lines, the close proximity of the running shed and fairly large goods yards and empty stock sidings each side of the running lines, there were always plenty of movements. Later on, I have tried to describe some of this activity for an hour or so at the beginning of the evening rush period. These busy periods occurred from time to time during the day as with any large main line junction station. I believe, during the latter days of steam in the 1950s and early 1960s, Guildford station was much favoured and frequented by enthusiasts of all ages though perhaps not to the extent that Tamworth was on the LMSR.

In 1925 the electric trains had already reached Guildford. These were the ex-LSWR

6  Guildford, showing lines to Reading (left) and Waterloo (right) (1985)

7  Guildford, showing Down lines to Portsmouth (1985)

third-rail pick-up units constructed from displaced steam rolling stock. The trains which normally consisted of three-car units, namely a motor coach at each end with a trailer car sandwiched between, used No. 1 bay platform. They travelled to Waterloo via Guildford (London Road) and Effingham Junction. At busy times two three-car units would be coupled together or two trailer cars would be placed in the centre with a three-car formation either side giving an eight-car train. Although we are only considering steam-hauled trains, I mention this electric service in order to give the reader an idea of how busy the station was.

Guildford was also the terminus for two push-pull services. These services were the branch trains to Horsham and those that ran to Farnham. The Horsham trains were often made up with two Marsh 'Balloon' coaches worked by a Central Section, ex-LBSCR, Stroudley D1 class 0–4–2T. The engine always propelled the train to Guildford and ran chimney first back to Horsham. With the huge Marsh 'Balloon' coaches towering over the D1 with its flat-topped cab, the general effect seemed to be rather comical.

The Reading and Redhill trains which passed through Guildford were stopping trains though some through goods trains hauled by N or U class Moguls passed through non-stop. In those days a variety of engine power was used on these trains between Redhill and Reading. For several years in the late twenties Stirling 4–4–0s of the F class with 7 ft driving wheels hauled most of the passenger trains. Later on, when the K class 2–6–4 tanks named after rivers on the Southern Railway were coming into service, the old Stirlings disappeared from the scene. On one occasion, the three-cylinder *River Frome*, No. A890, appeared for a whole week on a late afternoon Redhill to Reading train. The smooth and effortless getaway up the 1 in 100 gradient soon after leaving Platform 7 towards Wanborough, in contrast to the apparent struggle that the old Stirling 4–4–0s had, was really fascinating. These trains, incidentally, were made up normally of only three long ex-SE&CR 'Birdcage' stock. The total weight of the train was possibly 100 tons, a mere featherweight for *River Frome* which had a tractive effort of 25,387 lb.

About this time a number of the two-cylinder 'Rivers' were working on the Redhill–Reading route and their prompt starting on the 1 in 100 run towards Wanborough was equally impressive. After the regrettable derailment between Dunton Green and Sevenoaks (Tubs Hill) beneath the Shoreham Lane overbridge, all the 'River' class were withdrawn from service and were later converted to 2–6–0 tender engines of the U class. No. A890 was converted to the U1 class. Some readers will recollect that it was the 5.00 p.m. Cannon Street to Folkestone express hauled by No. A800 *River Cray* which was derailed. After a long enquiry and tests with a 'River' class engine on the LNER main line to York, it was decided that the track near Sevenoaks was at fault. Strangely enough, nearly 37 years later I was talking one day to a retired driver from the Southern Railway at Ashford, Kent, discussing the erstwhile 'River' class. Our discussion led inevitably to the Sevenoaks accident. It transpired that this driver was a fireman at the time of the accident and a few days before the accident had fired *River Cray* on the identical train. He could not remember a lot about the riding of the engine but he did recollect that it was a tough trip for the fireman. The train was timed to reach Ashford non-stop 65 minutes after leaving Cannon Street, an average of nearly 51 mph for the 55 mile run. Before leaving the subject of these engines, it always seemed to me that the policy of naming engines after rivers was rather weak and unimaginative. The old London & North Western Railway had many really splendid names for their engines such as *Hotspur*, *Comet*, *Leviathan*, *Swift*, *Mammoth*, *Colossus* and *Vulcan*.

Having been diverted by talk of the 'Rivers', I should now like to return to the subject of Guildford station and describe in some detail what happened between 4.15 p.m. and 5.30 p.m. on weekdays. It was a particularly interesting hour or so. There were naturally other times when similar activity was packed into a short space of time but the period I mention is one for which I have some notes and some vivid recollections.

At 4.32 p.m. a two-coach push-pull set propelled by an M7 0–4–4T would leave for Farnham from Platform 5. While this was happening, the 3.50 p.m. Waterloo to Portsmouth non-stop restaurant car express would tear through Platform 3 hauled as a general rule by a 'King Arthur' 4–6–0. On one occasion an S15 4–6–0 headed this train and sometimes a T9 4–4–0. Strangely enough, I never saw a U class or a U1 class on this train although a number of these Moguls were shedded both at Nine Elms and at Fratton. I did see a rebuilt Drummond T14 4–6–0 on this train but it was most unusual. Between 1923 and 1931, many of these T14 'Paddleboxes' were working to and from Portsmouth but they were not generally utilized for the fastest trains. After the 3.50 p.m. express from Waterloo had vanished into the tunnel at the western end of Guildford station, the station pilot No. E595, a 4–4–0 of the Adams X2 class, would move up to the eastern end of Platform 2 ready to propel the coaches of a slow train, the 3.24 p.m. from Waterloo which had now arrived at Platform 1, to the carriage sidings on the Down side beyond Platform 1. The train engine of this arrival was almost invariably a 'Small Hopper', a small-wheeled Drummond 4–4–0. Very occasionally, an Adams 0–4–2 of the A12 'Jubilee' class would arrive with this train. The engine, having been uncoupled, would proceed to the coaling stage near Platform 7 as soon as the express already mentioned had gone by.

Next, the Stroudley D1 with its two-coach push-pull set would move out of Platform 7 where it had arrived at 4.16 p.m. and cross over to the line for Platform 3. There the engine would have its water tanks refilled. With Westinghouse brake pump thumping occasionally, the train would remain there until 5.02 p.m. when it departed to Horsham. At 4.46 p.m. a semi-fast train for Waterloo would run into Platform 5. The train was usually loaded to seven or eight ex-LSWR non-corridor coaches in charge of a D15 4–4–0 or a T9. I remember an Adams X2 4–4–0 hauling this train on one occasion. The slowly revolving 7 ft 1 in driving wheels, the movement of the outside connecting rods and the subdued exhaust as she took off with a complete absence of slipping is something I can still remember. She was a lovely sight but unfortunately I do not have a record of her number. At 4.50 p.m. the Tonbridge to Reading train would arrive at Platform 7. For years a Stirling 7 ft F class 4–4–0 would be the normal engine but as I have already mentioned K class 2–6–4 tanks appeared around 1927. These were later displaced by D class 4–4–0s, many of which were in their original unsuperheated condition. The old Stirling 4–4–0s seemed a bit short of power when pulling away from Platform 7 with its 1 in 100 climb soon after the end of the platform, en route for Reading. However, they never slipped and to my knowledge never failed; they were just slow starters, and the large driving wheels didn't help. To my recollection some of these old Stirlings lasted well into 1945 and 1946 so, even if they were a little slow and underpowered, they must have been reliable, well-made and economical engines.

By 4.55 p.m. a Waterloo to Petersfield train would be due into Platform 1. This was the 4.15 p.m. fast to Guildford, then calling at all stations to Petersfield. Although the train was loaded to six or seven ex-LSWR non-corridor coaches, it was always a turn for one of the M7 Drummond 0–4–4 tanks. The first of the London commuters would leave this train at Guildford and the last of the returning school children would join it. This was always a well-loaded train.

In the meantime, the station pilot No. E595 had been busy shunting empty coaches while in the distance the famous roundhouse was a hive of activity. The Hawthorn-Leslie 0–4–0ST shed pilot, either *Ironside* or *Clausentum* of the 0458 class, was moving engines in or out of the shed. No. E458 *Ironside* was still at Guildford in December 1953 while No. E734 *Clausentum* went to Eastleigh. A picture of the latter engine appears on page 48. Coaling and watering was also proceeding near Platform 7 and some shunting in one of the goods yards, generally by G6 0–6–0 tanks, Adams 0–4–2 'Jubilees' or Adams 0–6–0s.

After a slight lull, the 5.28 p.m. arrival from Waterloo would run majestically into Platform 1. This was a corridor train complete with restaurant car and loaded up to ten coaches. Oddly, this train was often hauled by an unrebuilt Drummond four-cylinder 4–6–0 of the T14 class known as 'Paddleboxes'. The enormous tender carried 5,800 gallons of water and always leaked over the tender bogies. Neither Eastleigh nor any of the running sheds overcame the problem. Sometimes the train was hauled by a 'King Arthur'. One day, a Brighton Atlantic No. B425 *Trevose Head* was in charge. This was a mystery for a Brighton engine on the Portsmouth Direct line was unheard of in those days. This 5.28 p.m. arrival was a heavily filled train and after Guildford called only at Godalming, Haslemere, Petersfield and Portsmouth & Southsea before terminating at Portsmouth Harbour. Also at 5.28 p.m., the 3.55 p.m. semi-fast restaurant car train from Portsmouth Harbour to Waterloo would arrive in Platform 5, generally behind a D15 4–4–0 or a 'King Arthur' 4–6–0.

I hope the foregoing has given readers an idea of how fascinating Guildford station was in those far-off days.

Leaving Guildford for Portsmouth, one was plunged into a long tunnel within 200 yards or so of the end of the platform. After a short distance in the open another shorter tunnel followed. Originally, there was only one long tunnel but part of the centre portion collapsed, so this section was converted into a cutting. The line is level here and 1½ miles from Guildford, Shalford Junction is reached. There the Redhill trains branched off to the left to enter South Eastern & Chatham Railway territory as it was up to the 1923 grouping. Half a mile further on the Horsham branch swung away to the left, contracting to single line almost immediately. That old London Brighton & South Coast Railway line has, alas, long since been lifted. Passing under a road bridge which carries the old London to Portsmouth road, Peasmarsh sidings appeared on the Up side. The petroleum depot here always seemed to have several of the brightly painted and spotless four-wheeled tanker wagons on hand. The line is now ascending at a modest 1 in 410 increasing to 1 in 301 to Farncombe station. This is a suburb of Godalming and the nearest station for Charterhouse School. Farncombe was another quite busy commuter station in the late twenties and still is I believe. There were some short sidings both on the Up and Down sides here but I never remember seeing anything more than the odd horse box or wagon in them. After a short spell at 1 in 468 down, followed by an equally brief 1 in 200 up, the main line swings right. At that point roughly ¼ mile south of Farncombe station, Godalming goods sidings used to bear away to the left. They were on the site of the old Godalming terminus station before the line was extended south to Havant. Another short drop of 1 in 200 on a left-hand bend and Godalming station is reached. During the late twenties and early thirties, the new Godalming station consisted merely of Up and Down platforms alongside the respective tracks, the two usual trailing crossovers between the running lines and two very short sidings on the Down approach side. Here again was another busy commuter station. In those days, a semi-fast train would reach Waterloo, 34½ miles, in 52 to 60 minutes. The best evening train from Waterloo, the 4.50 p.m., took 50 minutes.

Immediately after leaving Godalming the line starts to curve to the right on a climbing gradient of 1 in 200. Down trains were faced with an eight-mile ascent, except for a short respite of ½ mile beyond Milford and ¾ mile past Witley, to within ½ mile of

8   Farncombe, looking towards Guildford (1937)

**9**  Station exterior, Godalming, on Down side (1938)

**10**  Godalming, with the Down line on the left (1937)

Haslemere. Over 60 years ago such a climb, most of it at 1 in 80 to 1 in 82, was hard work for an engine with nine or ten corridor coaches well packed with passengers and luggage. On many of the faster trains the formation included a restaurant car. The most powerful engines available then were the 'King Arthur' 4–6–0s, the similar H15 and S15 classes which had smaller driving wheels and the U class 2–6–0s. The then new 'Lord Nelson' class were all used, apart from odd running-in turns, on the West of England lines exclusively. The ten 'Schools' class 4–4–0s which were in service by 1931 were very new and did not come to the Portsmouth line until the middle thirties prior to electrification in 1937. The next most powerful engines were a few T14 4–6–0s, the ten D15 4–4–0s and the T9 4–4–0s. In 1931, though, the newly constructed three-cylinder U1 2–6–0s were sent to the Portsmouth line.

Returning now to the 1 in 200 climb out of Godalming, an overbridge carries the line over the old Portsmouth road from London. The track is now level for ¼ mile and passed Busbridge Sidings on the Down side. These consisted of a short siding for a local gravel company and a refuge siding. Very soon, the line is uphill at 1 in 100 to just before Milford, 36½ miles from Waterloo. Milford station is actually on a decline of 1 in 630. In the late twenties and early thirties, there were several sidings on the Up side, mainly for coal merchants, but also two gated sidings for the Hambledon Rural District Council. There was a level-crossing at the south end of the platforms and the signal-box was close by. The same falling gradient went on for ½ mile beyond Milford and after passing Great Enton lakes abruptly changed to a 1 in 82 rise for 1¼ miles until just before Witley. This

11   Milford. Down side on left (see also photograph 73) (after 1937)

short climb was a foretaste of what lay ahead and steam trains not stopping at Milford put on speed just before Milford station. At the time I am describing there were only a few London commuters using Milford and it was the first real country station on the line from Waterloo. Nowadays, of course, London-bound commuters in large numbers come from as far down the line as Petersfield.

Passing beneath the A283 road from Petworth to Milford, firemen had a short break from just before Witley with one mile falling at 1 in 122 then 1 in 93 before a 3¼ mile uphill slog at 1 in 80 up to Haslemere. Witley station was built on a long curve and in those days seemed to be in the middle of nowhere, being a mile or more from Witley village, and at least that distance from the three other villages in the vicinity. From late 1923 onwards, Witley station had several sidings, a goods shed and crane on the Down side and a short siding and cattle dock on the Up side. When I travelled on this line over 60 years ago, Down trains calling at Witley often backed into the sidings to detach or pick up one or more horse boxes. I do not know whether the horse age lingered on in that locality but an awful lot of people there seemed to have horses delivered by rail.

Steam trains calling at Witley then made a fairly sharp getaway for the assault on the 3¼ miles at 1 in 80 towards Haslemere. The start of this climb was ¾ mile ahead just after milepost 39. For over two miles the line curved gently through woods from which the sound of the locomotive exhaust echoed back. There was never any question of having a banking engine on this climb. Certainly I never heard of one and examination of old

12   Witley. Down side on left (after 1937)

**13**  Witley. As in photograph 12, but nearer signal-box

working timetables shows no mention of banking engines. All the way up this stiff climb until about ½ mile before Haslemere passing the village of Grayswood, the scenery was wooded, hilly and beautiful. Shortly before reaching Haslemere some of the fast trains of nine or ten coaches hauled by a 'King Arthur' or a U class Mogul would be down to 15 or 20 mph. A photograph of U class No. A624 taken in 1931 shows a heavy restaurant car train behind the engine which is obviously working hard (see photograph 79). The picture was taken two miles north of Haslemere about a mile from the summit of the climb. At summer weekends a regular procession of such trains followed each other at intervals up this bank. It was rather surprising that Witley to Haslemere was then a complete block section of about five miles. Half a mile from Haslemere the railway enters a fairly deep cutting. The line is level and quickly starts dropping at 1 in 100. The firemen then had an easier time for the next 12½ miles were downhill except for two very short up gradients.

Haslemere, 43 miles from Waterloo, was a good-sized country station and even 60 years ago had a sizeable number of commuters for Guildford and Waterloo. There were three platforms, a goods yard and shed with crane on the Down side and on the Up side were coal merchants' sidings. Each side of the line had a long shunting neck. Several passenger trains from Waterloo or Guildford terminated at Haslemere. There was no turntable so the engines of terminating trains were usually Drummond M7 0–4–4 tanks.

Leaving Haslemere, the line falls on a gradient of 1 in 100 for 1½ miles, easing to 1 in 231 and 1 in 690 to just before milepost 46. A mile rise at 1 in 250 changing to 1 in 279

**14** Haslemere. Up train hauled by U1 class entering station

down brings the line across the Surrey/Hampshire border to Liphook station. The station is 47 miles from Waterloo and a bit inconveniently situated from the village. Liphook has expanded since the early thirties though and many people commute to Waterloo now. In the late twenties and thirties it was merely a small country station. With another 8 miles of downhill running, except for the mile rise near Sheet Crossing shortly before Petersfield, fast trains tore through Liphook at between 60 and 70 mph. A good vantage point was where the railway crossed over the London to Portsmouth road about a mile south of Liphook. The station is actually on the falling gradient as one travels towards Portsmouth. The long refuge siding on the eastern or Down side of the station was therefore fitted with catch points. A similar siding to the west of Liphook station was placed on the Up side. Still on the Up side but east of the station were several goods sidings, a goods shed and a long shunting loop.

Beyond Liphook the line falls more gently curving slightly right and then left towards Liss Forest. The last two miles to Liss fall more sharply at 1 in 80. There were the usual goods sidings at Liss together with a goods shed and cattle pen. A refuge siding on the Up side of the station but west of the level-crossing had catch points fitted even though the exit was on an up gradient. Presumably, this was to protect the level-crossing.

**15** Liphook. Down side on left (1987). See photograph 89, taken at the same platform (1937)

**16** Liphook. Up side on left.

17    General view of Liss, with a Down EMU for Portsmouth at platform (1937)

Readers will wonder why no mention has been made of the Longmoor Military Railway which one always associated with Liss. In 1926, the LMR, or the Woolmer Instructional Military Railway as it was then known, had only just started its advance from Longmoor towards Liss. It did not reach Liss until 1933. In 1935, the WIMR was renamed the LMR. No rail connection was made with the Southern Railway until December 1942. The LMR closed in 1967 and the track was lifted in 1971. Liss thus returned almost to its pre-1933 state of semi-somnolence after 38 years of association with the Military Railway.

Another 4 miles of modest falling gradient, with one mile in between rising at 1 in 115, and Petersfield, 55 miles from Waterloo, is reached. There were five level-crossings between Liss and Petersfield, details of which are shown in the track layout plans in

18    Petersfield. On the old platform for Midhurst (before 1937)

19    Petersfield. Midhurst branch (closed) entering from left (after 1937)

**20** Petersfield, November 1985.
See photograph 88 for a similar view
(1937)

Appendix I. The station at Petersfield in steam days always seemed a long sprawling place to me. It is, however, well placed for the centre of the town. The Midhurst branch was served by a single platform which was rather awkwardly placed since it was separated from the main line platforms by a level-crossing. The Up and Down goods yards sidings extended well to the Portsmouth side of the station. There were also two sidings opposite the Midhurst branch platform. Up to July 1929, there was a small turntable in the Up side yard. Certain main line trains, both passenger and goods, either started or terminated at Petersfield and this would account for the then lavish run-round facilities.

About half a mile from Petersfield station still on a falling gradient of 1 in 273 the line swings almost due south. In another mile, before climbing to the summit of the South Downs in Buriton tunnel three miles from Petersfield, the railway swings south-east. About ¼ mile before the tunnel is entered from Petersfield, Buriton Signal Box, long since closed, stood on the Down side almost opposite the Buriton Lime Works sidings. The sidings were closed some 30 years ago but traces are still visible. Buriton tunnel is 485 yards in length and as Down trains emerged on the south side, the track became virtually downhill, or level, for the next 15½ miles right into Portsmouth. Unfortunately, the line is by no means straight for the next 7 miles as it squeezes through gaps in the South Downs. Really high speeds were therefore not usual in steam days. However, it was a break for the fireman. For Up trains, the 8 mile climb from Havant to Buriton tunnel could be difficult. Reference to the gradient profile will show that the last three

**21**  Rowlands Castle. Up side to Petersfield

miles at 1 in 100 to 1 in 80 up to the tunnel, and on a curving line too, was a stiff task with a heavy train especially if the rails were wet. This reminds me of an incident a life-long railwayman on the LSWR and Southern Railway related to me. He was in an Up train from Havant en route for Guildford one early autumn morning. The engine was a Drummond T9 4–4–0 and a severe bout of slipping took place on Buriton bank. The sanders were not sufficient so the poor fireman had to shovel sand under the driving wheels which eventually began to gain adhesion. All this on one of the hardest parts of the line for the fireman.

The next station is Rowlands Castle about 8½ miles from Petersfield. The village of Rowlands Castle is almost a suburb not only of Portsmouth but also of Havant, yet still maintains a country atmosphere. Like all the other small stations on the line from Woking, Rowlands Castle had a small goods yard. It also had two additional sidings on the south side of the station, one on the Up side and one on the Down side. The Associated Brick & Tile Company had two small gated sidings as well just before the station on the Up side.

Another three miles further on, all either on a falling or level gradient, brings the railway into Havant. After it passed Havant North signal-box, closed 3 November 1935, the junction was made with the old LBSCR line at a point 66¼ miles from Waterloo. The track now ran due west towards Portsmouth. This junction was the spot where congestion began for the remaining 8¼ miles to Portsmouth Harbour.

Havant station had two main line platforms and a third platform for the exclusive use

**22**   Havant, looking towards Portsmouth (1937)

**23**   Demolition of the old station, Havant (1938)

**24**   Havant. View from London end (1947)

**25**   Station exterior at Havant (1947)

of the branch trains running to and from Hayling Island. There was a fair-sized goods yard, a goods shed and a cattle dock here. On the side of the station used by the Hayling Island trains was a run-round loop and two short sidings. Examination of the station layout plan in Appendix I shows that soon after 1936 there were sizeable alterations to the station layout and not least to the signalling arrangements. The line from Havant towards Port Creek Junction is virtually level with no gradients of any note. This was line laid down by the LBSCR. Bedhampton Halt, just before Farlington Junction, was served by Central Section trains only. Farlington Junction is the eastern of the three junctions forming a triangle here. The north-western junction is Cosham and the south-western one is Port Creek. Trains making for the Salisbury, Bournemouth or Southampton direction from Havant left the main line at Farlington Junction and proceeded via Cosham Junction. The third side of the triangle from Cosham to Port Creek Junction marked the end of the old LSWR line from Fareham to Portsmouth. However, the LSWR and the LBSCR worked the line from Cosham to Portsmouth as a joint line.

All along the line from Farlington Junction to Fratton, the next large station, were several sidings for such bodies as the local gas works, the Admiralty and Bedhampton corn mill. There were also many crossings. After 73 miles from Waterloo, Fratton station was reached. There were three platforms here but surprisingly, until 1937, only one Up and one Down line served this busy station.

A level run of ³/₄ mile from Fratton brought trains into Portsmouth & Southsea station. In the period from 1923 to 1937, this station possessed five low-level terminal platforms

26  Portsmouth & Southsea. General view of low-level station (before 1923)

27    Portsmouth & Southsea. View of low- and high-level stations (before 1937)

28    Portsmouth & Southsea. As in photograph 27, but also showing Greetham Street Goods

29  Portsmouth & Southsea. An early view of the impressive main station building (*c.* 1910)

and two high-level platforms, actually an island platform with two edges in use. Trains going on to Portsmouth Harbour had a short climb at 1 in 61 to the high-level platform.

Portsmouth & Southsea station was opened by the LBSCR in June 1847 but was then called Portsmouth Town. The goods yard was on the south side of the station and was known as Greetham Street Goods. There were two goods running lines between the goods yard and Fratton station. One of these lines was converted to a passenger train line shortly before electrification in 1937. Because of the chronic congestion which occurred between Havant and Portsmouth & Southsea stations on summer Saturdays, it was incredible that the conversion of one goods line to passenger train working was not done at least twenty years earlier. On the north side of the station there was a small turntable and four short sidings. A loop line with run-round facilities led to three very short platforms. These platforms were presumably for the use of van trains or for transfer of heavy General Post Office mail at Christmas pressure periods when there were many extra van trains running.

Many Down trains terminated at Portsmouth & Southsea but all the restaurant car expresses from Waterloo went on to Portsmouth Harbour station, as did the ordinary express trains, since a steamer service to the Isle of Wight was part of the service. These trains carried destination boards labelled 'Waterloo, Portsmouth, Isle of Wight'. Portsmouth Harbour station was also the starting point and terminus for a number of long-distance trains to and from such places as Newcastle-on-Tyne, Liverpool, Cardiff,

York, Birmingham and Plymouth. Some of the long-distance trains used the Portsmouth & Southsea station as a terminus and starting point. As an aside, it is good to know that all these trains, and others, are still running. In 1985 I caught, on three separate occasions, a train from Portsmouth Harbour which was running right through to Weston-super-Mare via Salisbury and Bristol. Each train arrived punctually at Salisbury, after a small number of intermediate stops, in a most creditable time. During the years 1923 to 1947 or later, I daresay that train was made up of six or seven of William Panter's beautifully constructed non-corridor coaches hauled by a Drummond T9 4–4–0 or by a 7 ft Adams X2 4–4–0. There was a comparable train shown in the 1927 timetable which left Portsmouth & Southsea at 2.8 p.m. calling at Salisbury by 4.13 p.m. en route for Bristol but it had more intermediate stops.

So, we leave Portsmouth & Southsea via the high-level station on the last ³/₄ mile of the journey to the end of the line. This was always a very slow end to the journey for there are two sharp curves and no less than six gradient changes varying from 1 in 61 to 1 in 621. The Harbour station is opposite Gosport to where there is a passenger ferry. There is a steamer service to Ryde for passengers to the Isle of Wight. The service has remained basically unchanged through the years and makes connection with the trains to and from Waterloo. The journey time from Portsmouth Harbour to Ryde Pierhead, passengers only, was 45 to 50 minutes in each direction. For anyone making the journey from Waterloo to Ventnor on the southern tip of the Isle of Wight, the sea trip between the two contrasting trains made an extremely pleasant interlude in the journey. With an adequate meal on the train from Waterloo, followed by an interesting trip on the island to look forward to after the sea crossing, the complete trip was one I often remember with fond and nostalgic memories. It is rather sad to realize that the Isle of Wight steam trains, always so beautifully clean, with splendid personal service from the stations' staff and train personnel, have gone for ever. The one remaining bright spot is the privately-owned steam railway based on Haven Street station which one hopes will be able to expand in the future.

Returning now to the high-level station at Portsmouth & Southsea and the last ³/₄ mile to the Harbour station, there used to be a small turntable with four radiating spurs at Burnaby Road just under ¼ mile from the high-level station on the Up side. The turntable and spurs were not used after June 1946. Prior to then, it was useful for turning small tank engines. It is possible that some of the smaller LBSCR 0–4–2 tender engines and the LSWR Adams A12 0–4–2 tender engines which worked in to Portsmouth Harbour station from 1923 to 1947 could have turned here. It would have saved a trip up to Fratton to turn and thereby afforded relief to an already congested line. The Harbour station is a substantial terminus with five platforms served by one Up and one Down line. In addition, there was a branch line near the start of Platform 1 leading to HM Dockyard. From Platform 5, another branch line led to HM Gun Wharf served by three sidings and a run-round loop. The Isle of Wight steamers were berthed below and behind the station concourse. A short walk off the latter and down a stairway brought passengers alongside the gangways leading to the steamers. Apart from some track and platform alterations, the station has remained much as it was nearly seventy years ago.

# Chapter Three

# LOCOMOTIVES

A round ninety engines were based at Guildford Running Shed between 1923 and 1937. The following classes comprised virtually the whole complement:

| Class | Designer | Type | Duties | Remarks |
|-------|----------|------|--------|---------|
| 700 | Drummond | 0–6–0 | Goods | Known as 'Black Motors' |
| 395 | Adams | 0–6–0 | Goods | Fitted with square cab windows |
| 496 | Adams | 0–6–0 | Goods | Carried circular cab windows |
| G6 | Adams | 0–6–0T | Shunting | |
| 0458 | – | 0–4–0ST | Shed pilot | Builders – Hawthorn Leslie |
| M7 | Drummond | 0–4–4T | Light passenger | Also worked some short-distance semi-fast trains |
| K10 | Drummond | 4–4–0 | Mixed traffic | Known as 'Small Hoppers' |
| L11 | Drummond | 4–4–0 | Mixed traffic | Known as 'Large Hoppers' |
| L12 | Drummond | 4–4–0 | Passenger | Except fast trains |
| T9 | Drummond | 4–4–0 | Passenger | |
| X2 | Adams | 4–4–0 | Station pilot | No. E595 1920s only |
| A12 | Adams | 0–4–2 | Mixed traffic | Known as 'Jubilees' |
| U | Maunsell | 2–6–0 | Mixed traffic | Arrived around 1930 |

The number of William Adams' engines surviving well into the thirties was quite remarkable. The 0–4–2s of the A12 class were numerous at Guildford and could be seen on stopping trains, both goods and passenger, up and down the whole line. One of the Guildford A12s No. E555 was fitted with vacuum and Westinghouse brakes for handling Brighton stock as required. At one time seven of this class were fitted with dual braking systems. Together with the 395 and 496 classes of 0–6–0s, the A12s handled most of the goods work. The heavier 700 class 0–6–0s handled the longer goods trains. There were ninety engines in the A12 class most of which were built in 1897. Adams clearly had great faith in this wheel arrangement for mixed traffic work. The popular name of 'Jubilee' referred to their introduction in the year of Queen Victoria's Diamond Jubilee.

While on the subject of Guildford Running Shed and its complement of engines, mention should be made of the location for the breakdown train. This was accommodated in the long siding between the sheds and the Up line emerging from St Catherine's tunnel (see track layout in Appendix I).

**30** H15 class 4–6–0s at Woking. No. E483 on West of England line goods, No. E477 with Portsmouth Harbour station train (1931)

**31** HI5 class No. E483 at Woking (1931)

**32**   Class L12 4–4–0 No. E433

**33**   *Lord Anson* 'Lord Nelson' class 4–6–0 No. E861

**34**  D15 4–4–0 No. E472 at Eastleigh (1932)

**35**  Shunting at Guildford. Class G6 0–6–0T No. E160 (1931)

36   K10 4–4–0 No. E141 at Guildford. See part of the roundhouse behind the engine (1932)

37   T3 4–4–0 No. E574 adjacent to Guildford coaling stage (1932)

The whole site was somewhat hemmed in by deep cuttings on two sides. Consequently, every engine moving in or out of the sheds had to cross the turntable. Today, the whole area and associated track work has gone. A high wire fence segregates the remaining running lines from the running shed complex, including the old coaling stage, which has long since been transformed into a massive station car park.

The fast Waterloo to Portsmouth expresses were in charge of Nine Elms or Fratton based engines, usually 'King Arthurs' but very occasionally a T9 or quite exceptionally one of the S15 class. In later days towards 1931, U or U1 class Maunsell Moguls handled some of the fast trains. This was especially noticeable on summer weekends when there were many additional fast and semi-fast trains, some running in more than one part. Generally, the fast trains ran non-stop from Waterloo to Portsmouth & Southsea station and terminated farther on at Portsmouth Harbour station where there was a connecting steamer to Ryde Pierhead, Isle of Wight. Similarly, the Up trains from the Harbour station called at Portsmouth & Southsea and then ran fast to Waterloo.

The daily 3.50 p.m. fast train from Waterloo to Portsmouth was a typical train scheduled to take 99 minutes to Portsmouth & Southsea, before terminating at Portsmouth Harbour station. Nearly all the 'King Arthur' class in the number range E736–55, 763–92 and Nos. 451, 452 and 457 were seen on this train over a period of five years to 1930. Those locomotives in the last batch, E793–805, were never seen on the Portsmouth Direct line. Presumably, this was because they were fitted with 4,000 gallon tenders with six wheels, whereas all the others had 5,000 gallon eight-wheeled

38   D1 0–4–2T No. B266 alongside Guildford running shed (1932)

**39**   G6 0–6–0T No. E269 at Guildford running shed (1932)

**40**   Class 0395 0–6–0 No. 3506 at Guildford coaling stage (1932)

41    The Guildford station pilot for several years in the late twenties. X2 class 4–4–0 No. 595 (later E595) at Nine Elms (1922)

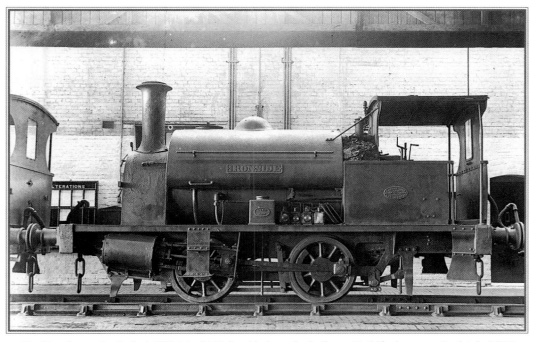

42    Hawthorne-Leslie 0–4–0ST No. 0458 *Ironside*, later shed pilot at Guildford, seen at Eastleigh (1923)

**43** No. 734 *Clausentum*, another Guildford shed pilot, also seen at Eastleigh (1931)

**44** V class 'Schools' 4–4–0 No. E903 *Charterhouse* visiting Farncombe (station for Charterhouse School), new, ex-works (1930)

**45** *Charterhouse* with close-up of valve gear. Note absence of smoke deflectors and omission of power/braking rating A at side of buffer beam above steps (1930)

tenders and would be unlikely to run low on water on this hilly 74 mile non-stop run. The Southern Railway was alone among the big four companies in having no water troughs anywhere on its system.

This absence of water troughs on the Southern seemed rather curious. Of the three constituent companies which made up the SR, the old LSWR with its longer mileage journeys would have benefitted most. The widespread use of the enormous eight-wheeled 5,000 and 5,800 gallon tenders, the latter for the T14 class, would have been unnecessary. Engine turning would have been simplified by greater use of turntables thus avoiding the use of triangles. Water troughs could have been laid on the level track between Guildford and Peasmarsh Junction where water was available from the River Wey. This was very roughly halfway between Waterloo and Portsmouth between mileposts 31 and 32.

Fratton, the only other running shed on the section of line with which we are concerned, stabled around seventy-five engines daily between 1923 and 1937. Not all these locomotives were required for the Portsmouth Direct line. Some were scheduled for work on the Central Section. The Portsmouth Direct line joined the old LBSCR line at Havant where Victoria to Portsmouth and Brighton to Portsmouth trains of the Central Section, ex-LBSCR, and Western Section, ex-LSWR, trains shared the line into Portsmouth. Other engines based at Fratton were needed for Bournemouth and Southampton trains via Fareham, to Eastleigh, to Salisbury, to the Meon Valley line, and for the Hayling Island and Midhurst branches. Locomotive classes represented at Fratton were:

| Class | Designer | Type | Duties | Remarks |
|---|---|---|---|---|
| *Ex-LSWR engines* | | | | |
| D15 | Drummond | 4–4–0 | Semi-fast passenger | All ten of the class were at Fratton at one time |
| T9 | Drummond | 4–4–0 | Semi-fast passenger | |
| M7 | Drummond | 0–4–4T | Slow passenger and push-pull trains | |
| 700 | Drummond | 0–6–0 | Goods | 'Black Motors' |
| 395 | Adams | 0–6–0 | Light goods | |
| A12 | Adams | 0–4–2 | Mixed traffic | 'Jubilees' |
| O2 | Adams | 0–4–4T | Light passenger trains | |
| *Ex-LBSCR engines* | | | | |
| K | L.B. Billinton | 2–6–0 | Mixed traffic | No. B342 was painted umber, B346 was black |
| C2X | D.E. Marsh | 0–6–0 | Goods | |
| A1X | Stroudley | 0–6–0T | Light passenger trains | 'Terriers' |
| D1 | Stroudley | 0–4–2T | Light passenger and push-pull trains | |
| B4X | R.J. Billinton | 4–4–0 | Semi-fast passenger | No. B201 had a steel firebox |
| E3 | R.J. Billinton | 0–6–2T | Light goods | |
| E4 | R.J. Billinton | 0–6–2T | Mixed traffic | |
| E1 | Stroudley | 0–6–0T | Light general work | |
| *From 1931 onwards for Portsmouth to Waterloo service* | | | | |
| U1 | Maunsell | 2–6–0 | Fast and semi-fast passenger | New from Eastleigh |
| *From 1935 to 1937* | | | | |
| V | Maunsell | 4–4–0 | Fast and semi-fast passenger | Ten 'Schools' class |

**46** *Charterhouse* in service later at Charing Cross (1931)

A small turntable was installed near Burnaby Road, Portsmouth, between the two Portsmouth stations in order to allow smaller engines from the Harbour station to turn without the need to return either to the Fratton triangle or to the Fratton turntable. This latter turntable was 50 feet in diameter and thus the biggest engine which it could turn was a U or U1 class Mogul. Longer engines such as the 'King Arthurs' and T9s fitted with eight-wheeled tenders had to use the Fratton triangle.

Up to the beginning of 1931 the Drummond D15 4–4–0s handled the semi-fast passenger trains almost exclusively. They were powerful, free-running engines which Fratton shed always kept splendidly clean. Except for the typical Drummond cab and separate driving wheel splashers, these engines always reminded me of Robinson's 'Directors' from the old Great Central Railway. No. E463, the first of the class which were numbered E463–72, was the last one to retain its Caledonian-type hooter in place of the normal LSWR whistle. When the class was new, all engines were fitted with the Caledonian-type hooter which sounded much the same as the later LMS hooter.

**47**   700 class 0–6–0 No. 316 on a Down goods near Petersfield (1936)

**48**   A1X 0–6–0T No. B661 at Fratton Yard (1931)

**49**   B4X 4–4–0 on the turntable inside Fratton shed (1928)

**50**   K 2–6–0 No. 2345 at Eastleigh (1931)

51   H2 4–4–2 No. B425 *Trevose Head* (1930)

52   E3 0–6–2T No. B167 (1927)

**53** E2 0–6–0T No. B103 (1930)

Evidently, Dugald Drummond brought this memento with him from the Caledonian Railway. These D15s, originally non-superheated, were superheated by R.W. Urie who succeeded Drummond after the latter's tragic death in 1913. The conversion to superheating was carried out to the whole class between 1915 and 1917. Occasionally, a T9 would handle a train which ran semi-fast from Waterloo to Guildford then all stations to Portsmouth. A photograph of a T9 on one of these trains appears on page 83. The non-corridor stock making up the train should be noted.

While on the subject of motive power for the slow and semi-fast trains on the line, I recall an incident in 1929 which took me by surprise. For a whole week, I was joining the 3.40 p.m. semi-fast from Waterloo due to leave Guildford at 4.32 p.m. and calling at all stations from Guildford to Portsmouth. This train was normally an M7 turn and only a four-coach non-corridor train. With the M7, the water tanks were replenished at Guildford and presumably topped up again at Petersfield. Imagine my surprise and delight at seeing newly built 'Lord Nelson' class No. E861 *Lord Anson* run smoothly into Platform 1 at Guildford punctually on the Monday. She was on a running-in turn. This was repeated every day of the week up to and including Friday. The quiet exhaust, eight beats per revolution of the driving wheels, was a revelation. The getaway from each station was almost up to electric train standard and, at times, sounded as if she was slipping so rapid were the exhaust beats. It was incidents such as this that made train travel so interesting in those days.

An unusual event took place at Farncombe station in 1930 which heralded the arrival

**54**   B4X 4–4–0 No. B56 at New Cross Gate (1926)

**55**   C2X 0–6–0 No. B440, single–dome version, at Battersea (1929)

56   K1 2–6–4T No. A890 *River Frome* at Bricklayers' Arms. This was the sole example of this class (1926)

57   K 2–6–4T No. A799 *River Test*

58    Rebuilt D1 4–4–0 No. 1747

59    N 2–6–0 No. A817 at Bricklayers' Arms (1926)

60    E1 4–4–0 No. A179 at Longhedge (1924)

61    F 4–4–0 No. A22 at Ashford (1927)

of the fourth of Maunsell's new V class 'Schools' three-cylinder 4–4–0s. *Charterhouse*, No. E903, arrived light early one Saturday morning in the small Up sidings at Farncombe. She was new from Eastleigh Works and was displayed mainly for the benefit of boys from Charterhouse School which is not far from Farncombe station. The picture on page 49 was taken at the time and shows the locomotive with the original small chimney and no smoke deflectors. Visitors that day were allowed a very thorough examination of the engine. *Charterhouse* was one of the original batch of ten engines which were later augmented by a further thirty. The 'Schools' later ran splendidly on the fast Waterloo to Portsmouth trains from 1935 up to the end of steam passenger trains between Waterloo and Portsmouth in July 1937 when electrification was extended to Portsmouth. Even so, goods, van trains, excursions and certain cross-country trains continued to be steam hauled right up to the final day of steam on the Southern. The 'Schools' were perhaps the finest all-round 4–4–0s ever built in this country and following the successful introduction of Maunsell's U1 three-cylinder 2–6–0s on the Portsmouth Direct line in 1931, the 'Schools' were obvious successors.

The U class Ashford Moguls started to appear on the line about 1927 or 1928, being joined by the newly built U1s in 1931. The latter engines were built at Eastleigh and numbered 1890 to 1909. This followed the 1930 numbering system whereby LSWR engines retained their numbers, ex-SE&CR engines added 1,000, ex-LBSCR locomotives added 2,000 and obsolete classes added 3,000. The three prefixes in use, 'E', 'A' and 'B' were dropped. Thus, the U1s could still be identified as Ashford engines. The U1s certainly improved the timekeeping on the semi-fast trains which by 1931 were becoming longer and heavier by reason of the introduction of a little corridor stock.

I well remember travelling on the 5.52 p.m. semi-fast Waterloo to Portsmouth train on numerous occasions. This train was fast to Guildford, next stop Haslemere, then Petersfield, and finally slow from Havant. The normal loading was six or seven non-corridor coaches. The 12½ miles between Guildford and Haslemere were scheduled at a generous 24 minutes even allowing for the long 1 in 80 climb between Witley and Haslemere. With a two-cylinder U class engine, an early arrival at Haslemere was a foregone conclusion but with a U1 engine it was a certainty. The ex-LSWR crews really got the best out of these engines. The 2–6–0s were, of course, relatively new at the time I am quoting.

Before the arrival of the Ashford Moguls, there were a number of semi-fast trains handled, surprisingly, by the Drummond M7s. A typical train was the 4.15 p.m. Waterloo to Petersfield. This train was fast to Guildford and then called at all stations to Petersfield. On one wintry evening the smokebox door of the M7 was not only red-hot but almost transparent as the train ran into Platform 1 at Guildford. I assume this was because the smokebox door was not properly secured. I forget whether the engine was changed or not. Engine changing did sometimes take place at Guildford but not as a regular practice.

The Drummond M7 tank engines were originally intended for semi-fast suburban trains and certainly between 1926 and 1931 they were often seen on the lighter loaded semi-fast trains between Waterloo and Guildford, or Waterloo and Haslemere, or even to Petersfield. They were quite powerful engines, tractive effort 19,755 lb, but with leading

62    Rebuilt B1 4–4–0 No. 1455 at Reading (1948)

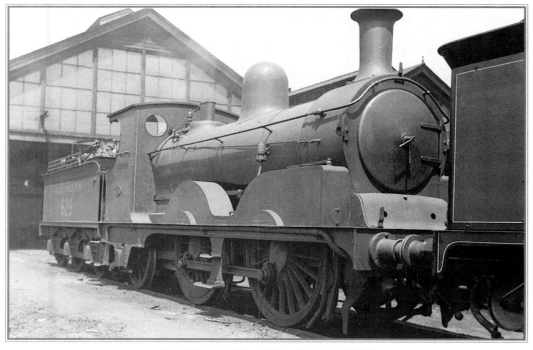

63    A12 0–4–2 No. E629 at Eastleigh (1934)

**64** 02 0–4–4T No. 227 (later E227) in LSWR finish at Strawberry Hill (1920)

**65** A12 0–4–2 No. 555 (later E555) in LSWR finish. Note Westinghouse brake fitted (1924)

**66**    The same engine as in photograph 65 in SR finish

**67**    Rebuilt T14 4–6–0 No. E447. Note massive 5,800 gallon tender

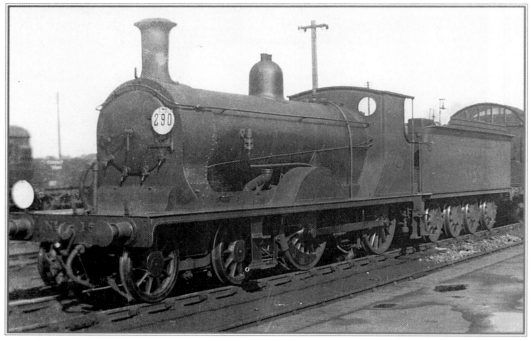

68   L11 4–4–0 No. E159. These mixed traffic engines normally had eight–wheeled tenders

69   S15 class 4–6–0 No. 501 (LSWR), later E501, on Down Portsmouth line goods

driving wheels, when running forwards, the choice of such duties for these engines seemed unusual. In 1921 the then Chief Mechanical Engineer of the LSWR, R.W. Urie, had M7 No. 126, later Southern Railway No. E126, superheated and the cylinders enlarged. This engine then remained in the London area for the rest of its service. It has been stated that the modifications raised the centre of gravity unduly thereby making the engine unsteady at speed. I have been unable to verify this but its use almost wholly on the movement of empty coaches in and out of Waterloo for many years seems logical if the engine had tended to be top heavy.

Readers might be interested in what happened to one of the three Drummond T9 locomotives shedded at Fratton in 1927. The three were Nos. E302, E337 and E338. One Saturday morning, No. E337 became derailed right outside Portsmouth Harbour station with every wheel of the engine and tender off the road. Unfortunately every track into and out of the station was blocked. Eight hours elapsed before the station could be used once more. A picture of the engine appears in photograph 80 on page 83 which was taken some four years later when it was still working on the Portsmouth line. Luckily, trains were able to use the nearby Portsmouth & Southsea station as a terminus.

Fratton was selected as the base for the ten 'Schools' class engines brought into use on the Portsmouth line in 1935. The engines concerned were:

| | |
|---|---|
| No. 924 | *Haileybury* |
| No. 925 | *Cheltenham* |
| No. 926 | *Repton* |
| No. 927 | *Clifton* |
| No. 928 | *Stowe* |
| No. 929 | *Malvern* |
| No. 930 | *Radley* |
| No. 931 | *King's Wimbledon* |
| No. 932 | *Blundells* |
| No. 933 | *King's Canterbury* |

Strangely, three of these ten are the only preserved 'Schools' class, Nos. 925, 926 and 928. The remainder of the class were cut up at Ashford during the early 1960s.

During 1935, there was a further acceleration in train times and some improvement in services mainly to ward off opposition from the motor coach companies. The fast trains between Waterloo and Portsmouth were timed at 90 minutes in place of the 98 minute timing. The success of the 'Schools' class was immediate. They were popular engines, not only with the footplate crews and the running shed staff, but also with the general public. The U1s and the D15s were gradually displaced to other duties and areas. The splendid work of the 'Schools' has been adequately written about by numerous people and there is no need for me to repeat their exploits on the Portsmouth line. I did, however, have the pleasure of travelling behind many of these engines which were shedded at Ramsgate between 1942 and 1945. I used to catch the 3.15 p.m. Charing Cross to Ramsgate via Ashford Down and the 7.16 a.m. Walmer to Cannon Street Up

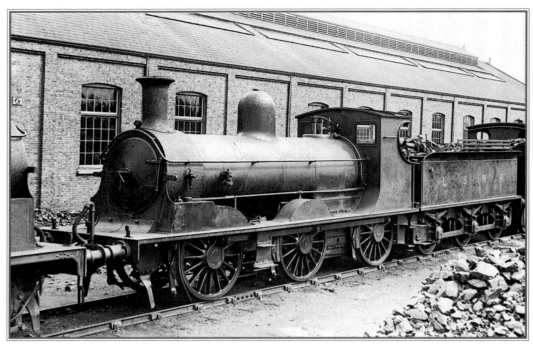

**70**    0395 class 0–6–0 No. 101 (LWSR), later E101, at Strawberry Hill (1921)

**71**    700 class 0–6–0 No. 326 (LWSR), later E326, at Nine Elms before being superheated (1922)

**72**    700 class 0–6–0 No. E325 in superheated form

**73**    U class 2–6–0 No. 1620 passing Milford with a very short van train (1937)

**74**  T14 class 4–6–0 No. E445 at Waterloo in original condition. Because water leaked from the tender tank over the bogies they were known as 'Paddleboxes.' See photograph 67 for a rebuilt T14

**75**  Haslemere. M7 tank on train at Platform 3

**76**   Woking. U class 2–6–0 No. A622 carriage shunting (1931)

trains regularly each week. The 7.16 a.m. started at Ramsgate. The morning train was slow to Ashford and then fast to Cannon Street where it was due at 9.38 a.m., 73 minutes after leaving Ashford. In spite of single line working between Martin Mill and Kearsney Junction outside Dover (the Up line was in use by the Army), perhaps a cross-channel shelling warning at Dover and V1 and V2 rockets nearer London, the timekeeping was fantastic, not to mention the valiant efforts to regain lost time which were often quite successful. Sometimes it was a case of V1 rockets, 'Doodle-bugs', versus V1 'Schools' and the latter came off best.

After July 1937, the ten 'Schools' class were reallocated. Some went to Bournemouth, some to Bricklayers' Arms, others to Ramsgate and one to Stewarts Lane. Many of the class were less than thirty years old when they were withdrawn and scrapped. One cannot help feeling that British Railways were hasty and thoughtless in their premature action to be rid of steam.

However, steam lingered on in reduced form until the end of the Southern Railway so far as the Portsmouth line was concerned. In Chapter Nine readers will be interested to learn of a Royal Train trip from Waterloo to Portsmouth Harbour and back, behind the 4–6–0 engine No. 850 *Lord Nelson* which took place in 1947.

*Chapter Four*

# PASSENGER ROLLING STOCK

The passenger rolling stock in use on the Portsmouth Direct line during the years from 1923 to 1937 was almost wholly ex-LSWR non-corridor compartment variety. There were corridor coaches in use on the fast trains and a few semi-fast trains only. Most of the stock dated from the 1890s, designed by William Panter and later improved by Surrey Warner. Bogie stock was almost universal but there were quite a number of six-wheeled brake/luggage vans still in use up to 1931. I do not ever remember seeing a six-wheeled passenger coach in use during this period. These had presumably been sold off to minor railways, downgraded to engineers' vehicles or broken up.

The provision of toilets, not only for first class, but also for third-class passengers, was liberal in these non-corridor coaches. Sometimes a toilet would be sandwiched between two compartments with a small side corridor connected to each compartment by end doors. In this case, the seating capacity of each compartment would be reduced from ten to nine in the third-class compartments. A transverse door in the small corridor led to the toilet. In other cases the toilet was parallel to the sides of the coach and a door led directly into a single compartment. Generally, every coach had one or two toilets,

Third-class compartments were well upholstered in black and red buttoned cloth of an uncut moquette type. The cushions and seat backs were stuffed with horsehair. Window blinds of the roller type, leather straps to raise or lower the door windows and sliding ventilators over the doors were among the fittings. Wooden railed racks with a tough string webbing or netting were provided, 'For light articles only', above the seats. The ceiling contained two additional adjustable ventilators and a large glass bowl containing two electric bulbs. These coaches were originally gas-lit and some such stock was still in use in the late twenties. At the terminal stations and the larger stations such as Guildford, there were a number of gas cylinder wagons in evidence in the carriage sidings. Recharging of gas cylinders beneath the coaches was carried out from these wagons.

Framed pictures above the backs of the seats showed views, mainly of beauty spots and seaside resorts served by the Southern Railway. The *pièce de résistance* was a large map of the complete Southern Railway system, also framed. All the now long-forgotten branches such as the Petersfield to Midhurst, Sandling Junction to Sandgate, Seaton Junction to Seaton, Basingstoke to Alton and Axminster to Lyme Regis were faithfully shown with all the intermediate stations or halts. Finally, a mirror generally on the opposite side of the compartment from the map, completed the furnishing. The overall interior colour scheme was, however, rather drab being that old Victorian favourite, a dingy dark brown paint. Brass fittings for the doors, such as handles and latches, smokers' assistants for striking Swan Vestas, for the roller blind 'keeps' and, last but not least, for the steam heating regulator handle, were used. Naturally, brass screws were used in the compartments. Nothing was skimped. Only in the third-class compartments was the floor covered with brown linoleum of a tough wearable quality. The steam heating was most effective and on a freezing winter morning with all windows shut and the heating system turned on to 'Full', it was pure luxury.

The first-class compartments were the acme of comfort. The seats were larger and softer, provided with folding armrests, antimacassars and carpets or thick mats. There were arm pulls for the corner passengers and the colour scheme was in lighter and more cheerful hues than the sombre colours of the third-class compartments.

Another interesting point was that the smoking compartments had the word 'Smoking' engraved on the glass at the side of the corner seats. There were also a number of compartments for 'Ladies only'. Such compartments were in the brake third coaches or, in the case of first-class coaches, reasonably close to the guard.

In all coaches, the communication cord was painted red and appeared above the corner seats. The warning notice stated: 'To stop the train pull down the chain. Penalty for improper use £5.' It seems to me that the present penalty of £50 is comparatively cheap compared with £5, say in 1930, for the average weekly wage was well below £5 for a man.

All these coaches had 'Mansel' wheels. The wheel was built up with wooden segments between the hub and the rim. As a result, the running was very quiet with a complete absence of 'ringing' associated with the perforated steel disc wheel fitted to more modern coaches. I should think that the excellent silent running of the very modern four-car-unit electric trains, which operate suburban stopping trains out of Waterloo, is comparable with the quiet running of the old 'Mansel' wheeled LSWR stock.

These old LSWR non-corridor coaches had slam locks to the doors unlike some of the contemporary SE&CR coaches which were fitted with handles needing two distinct partial turns to lock them. These latter handles could be likened to a flattened letter 'O' in the horizontal position when locked. Some of the LBSCR coaches had similar door handles to those of the SE&CR.

The LSWR corridor coaches were all of the compartment type with side corridors. A toilet was provided at each end of the coach. In the case of the brake third corridor coaches, a toilet was provided at the compartment end of the vehicle. These corridor coaches were of later construction than the bogie compartment non-corridor vehicles and, though they were only fractionally longer, weighed over 30 tons compared with 26 to 28 tons for the non-corridor coaches. The general standard of fittings and appointments was similar to the older compartment stock. The corridor stock had, of course, the restaurant car variation. The ex-LSWR corridor stock was also easily recognizable by their large external bogie frame and variation in the suspension arrangements.

In Chapter Six, dealing with passenger train running, it will be noted that on summer Saturdays there was an absolute procession of restaurant car trains up and down the line. A fair number of vehicles had thus to be prepared for use both from Waterloo and from Portsmouth.

The make-up of slow trains terminating at Guildford, Haslemere or Petersfield was normally four bogie non-corridor coaches. A brake third at either end with a third and first sandwiched between was typical. Sometimes, two first and third composites would be placed in the middle of the two brake thirds. It was not unusual in the late twenties and early thirties for a six-wheeled brake/luggage van to take the place of one brake third. In that case, an extra third or third and first composite would be inserted making the train up to five vehicles.

| Seats | | | Length | Width | Vehicles in Stock |
|---|---|---|---|---|---|
| *Non-Corridor Bogie Stock (as at 1 January 1924)* | | | | | |
| *3rd Class* | | | | | |
| 1. | 76 | 8 compartments, 4 with lavatories | 59 ft 7 in | 8 ft ³/₄ in | 37 |
| 2. | 38 | 4 compartments (Brake 3rd), 2 with lavatories | 59 ft 7 in | 8 ft ³/₄ in | 74 |
| 3. | 78 | Saloon, push-pull | 59 ft 7³/₄ in | 8 ft 6 in | 3 |
| 4. | 64 | Saloon, push-pull | 51 ft 10 in | 8 ft 6 in | 2 |
| 5. | 74 | 8 compartments, 2 with lavatories | 58 ft 0 in | 8 ft ³/₄ in | Not available |
| *Corridor Bogie Stock* | | | | | |
| *3rd Class* | | | | | |
| 6. | 64 | 8 compartments, 2 end lavatories | 59 ft 7 in | 8 ft 6³/₄ in | 35 |
| 7. | 64 | 8 compartments, 2 end lavatories | 60 ft 7 in | 9 ft 0 in | 16 |
| 8. | 64 | 8 compartments, 2 end lavatories | 60 ft 7 in | 8 ft 6³/₄ in | 16 |
| *Southern Railway Stock* | | | | | |
| *Non-Corridor Bogie Stock (as at 1 January 1935)* | | | | | |
| *3rd Class* | | | | | |
| 1. | 90 | 9 compartments | 61 ft 7 in | 8 ft ³/₄ in | 4 |
| *(As at 1 January 1937)* | | | | | |
| 2. | 88 | 9 compartments, 2 with lavatories | 61 ft 7 in | 8 ft ³/₄ in | 38 |
| 3. | 72 | 8 compartments, 4 with lavatories | 61 ft 7 in | 8 ft ³/₄ in | 12 |

Ex-LSWR Passenger Stock

Although restaurant car trains were in great use at this time for the fast trains, there were some semi-fast trains loaded up to eight or even ten vehicles, all of them non-corridor coaches. This was quite normal at holiday times when presumably every serviceable vehicle was pressed into use.

Readers may like to have some data on the ex-LSWR passenger stock which was in use in the late twenties, as well as some details of early Southern Railway stock introduced in the early thirties, for comparison. The table opposite shows the principal measurements and number of vehicles in stock at various census dates between January 1924 and January 1937. The list is not comprehensive and covers only a representative selection of stock. Apart from two push-pull coaches there was very little variation in the overall length over the buffers, most vehicles being within the range 59 ft 7 in to 61 ft 7 in.

There were also large numbers of so-called 'Converted stock' in the Southern Railway passenger stock records. The standard vehicle length fell within the range already quoted, while width fell in the range quoted above. Much of the converted stock had only slight internal differences and the number of compartments varied from 7 to 8 with 4 for a brake. Most of these coaches appeared to be of William Panter's original design.

*Chapter Five*

# GOODS TRAIN RUNNING

<hr>

What we now term a freight train was always known as goods or goods train during the era up to 1945. I think that goods trains became known as freight trains after the end of the Second World War. About that time lorries were often called trucks, from American influence during the war no doubt.

All railway enthusiasts know that the Southern Railway was first and foremost a passenger line and very much a holidaymakers' line. Goods traffic there was but it took very much a second place. Certainly a goods train as we knew it in, say, 1927 looked very different from a present-day freight train or freightliner. There were of course long-distance fast goods trains made up of vacuum-fitted stock but such trains were rare on the Southern whereas on the old LMS, LNER, and GWR, there were many such trains timed to run at little short of express passenger or semi-fast passenger train speeds. The Western Section of the Southern in general, and the Woking to Portsmouth line in particular, had a fair number of short-distance goods trains. The main goods depots between Woking and Portsmouth were at Guildford, Godalming and Petersfield. Haslemere was well supplied with sidings, cattle dock, crane and goods shed. Every intermediate station on the line had a few sidings even Farncombe which was mainly a commuter station. Some stations had a cattle dock and provision for handling horse boxes. These horse boxes could be likened to a four-wheeled version of the old LSWR six-wheeled brake/luggage vans. There was a half-compartment at one end for the attendant groom while the remainder of the vehicle accommodated the horse. The general outside appearance closely resembled the non-corridor passenger stock designed by William Panter.

There were no fast fitted goods trains running between Nine Elms and Portsmouth or between Woking and Portsmouth on a regular schedule. Such trains as there were of this type were specially run as required. The slow pick-up or local goods train was very much in evidence on the Portsmouth line. Most of these trains started at Guildford and ran to Woking, Godalming, Haslemere or Petersfield. There were similar trains in the reverse direction. In addition there were a number of trains running from Petersfield to Portsmouth. Guildford was undoubtedly the busiest station for goods traffic on the line. As well as the Up and Down goods trains on the main line, trains were despatched to Horsham, Clandon on the electric line to Waterloo via Effingham Junction, Farnham, Reading and Redhill. Many Reading to Redhill goods trains passed through Guildford leaving the Portsmouth Direct line at Shalford Junction, 1½ miles south of Guildford station.

The distribution of loco coal for the Woking to Portsmouth line was particularly interesting. The supply came from Aberdare in Glamorgan and was conveyed in Stephenson & Clarke's wagons direct to Woking, Guildford and Fratton. The empty wagons were returned to Aberdare via Salisbury marshalled together, care being taken to ensure that other traders' empty wagons were kept entirely separate. As coal trains went direct to Fratton via Salisbury or to Guildford via Woking, the long climb of 1 in 80 between Witley and Haslemere was avoided.

Another notable goods working was that of cattle traffic from the Northern lines to Guildford and similar traffic from Chichester to Guildford. A big cattle market was, and presumably still is, held in Guildford. Northern lines cattle traffic was worked specially from Woking to Guildford when necessary with arrangements made by Woking. Similar traffic from Chichester market was worked into Fratton. From there, traffic for stations from Guildford to Witley inclusive were worked via Eastleigh and Woking. For stations from Rowlands Castle to Haslemere, trains worked direct from Fratton.

Some of the operating instructions, dated 1926, for slow goods trains working the line between Woking and Portsmouth make quite fascinating reading today. I list some of the details for operating personnel:

### 6.4 a.m. Guildford to Godalming (Goods)

Should the train start before arrival of the 2.10 a.m. goods from Nine Elms, latter train will stop at Farncombe to detach and place in Down siding wagons for Godalming. Shunting operations to be carried out at Farncombe under personal supervision of Stationmaster, who will arrange for Godalming Goods to fetch the wagons.

[As Farncombe was the first stop on the Down line after Guildford, for goods traffic the unfortunate stationmaster had to be prepared for a start soon after 6.00 a.m. at short notice. E.J.R.].

### 11.20 a.m. Guildford to Petersfield (Not Saturdays)

Guildford to provide heavy brake van when the train is required to call at Busbridge siding. It will stop at Godalming to take up a shunter. It must be shunted into the refuge siding at Busbridge before attaching and detaching wagons. Godalming to advise Guildford when this arrangement is necessary and arrange for the siding to be kept open for the reception of the train.

### 11.51 a.m. Guildford to Woking

Guildford to advise Woking by 11.00 a.m. the number of wagons required to connect with the 2.43 p.m. goods, Woking to Basingstoke.

### 3.6 p.m. Guildford to Woking

The load of this train from Guildford must not exceed 40 vehicles including van.

### 7.57 p.m. Guildford to Petersfield (Tuesdays only)

This train will only stop at intermediate stations shown if there is any traffic to be detached, and will run as far as required, but not beyond Petersfield.

N.B. Conveys any other traffic on hand at Guildford for the Portsmouth Direct line.

*9.26 p.m. (Not Saturdays) 8.40 p.m. (Saturdays only) Haslemere to Guildford*

Milford and Witley to advise Haslemere only the number of wagons to be attached.

*5.40 p.m. (Not Saturdays) Petersfield to Guildford*

Nine Elms wagons to be kept together on the train.

*6.35 p.m. Petersfield to Fratton*

Will run on Wednesdays only (Petersfield Market Day). Heavy brake van to be provided at rear. Stops at Rowlands Castle if required. Cattle from Petersfield to Fareham, Gosport etc., will be worked from Fratton to Portsmouth and there attached to the 8.28 p.m. goods. Portsmouth to arrange and advise all concerned.

*7.40 a.m. Woking to Guildford*

Stops at Worplesdon to detach wagons and for Road Box traffic.
[Road Box traffic probably referred to small containers carried on four-wheeled flat wagons by rail and transferred to flat lorries at Worplesdon. E.J.R.]

*12.33 p.m. Woking to Guildford*

Traffic for South Eastern Section to be marshalled next engine.

*2.50 p.m. (Not Saturdays) Woking to Godalming*

*2.50 p.m. (Saturdays only) Woking to Guildford*

The load of this train not to exceed 55 wagons and brake van on arrival at Guildford.

## MARSHALLING OF CERTAIN GOODS TRAINS ON WEEKDAYS

The above is the heading for a section of the working timetable dealing with goods trains. The order in which wagons had to be marshalled in relation to the engine was regarded as vital by the operating staff. A little thought will show that if the wagons are carefully positioned in any train where the number of wagons and vans might be sixty or more, unnecessary shunting movements can be avoided at intermediate stations where vehicles have to be detached or attached. Moreover, the train may be more easily dealt with at its destination particularly when the train has to be divided.

I give three examples of marshalling (formation) instructions for 1926:

*11.51 a.m. (Not Saturdays) Guildford to Woking*

Engine; wagons for Woking and east of Woking; wagons for stations west of Woking; van.

*11.55 a.m. Guildford to Woking*

Formation leaving Guildford: engine; wagons for Down line stations via Woking; wagons for Up line stations via Woking; wagons for Nine Elms; van.

*8.35 p.m. Woking to Guildford*

Engine; wagons for stations Shalford to Reigate inclusive; wagons for other SE&C Section's stations; wagons for Guildford; wagons for Portsmouth Direct line; wagons for Tongham [Farnham line]; van.

A number of goods trains had to be worked with heavy goods brake vans. The reasons were either because the number of wagons was high, perhaps up to sixty vehicles or more, or because the train would traverse the steepest parts of the line, e.g. between Witley and Haslemere or from Petersfield to Havant.

The following details are taken from the working timetable for the year 1927:

*Summary of Goods Trains Worked with Heavy Goods Brake Vans*

|  |  | HGBV Type | No. |
|---|---|---|---|
| 11.40 a.m. | Godalming Goods to Guildford | N | 53 |
| 1.25 p.m. | (Saturdays only) Godalming Goods to Guildford | N | 20 |
| 7.20 p.m. | (Not Saturdays) Godalming Goods to Guildford | N | 20 |
| 6.4 a.m. | (Not Mondays) Guildford to Godalming Goods | N | 53 |
| 11.20 a.m. | (Not Saturdays) Guildford to Petersfield | O | 26 |
| 5.40 p.m. | (Not Saturdays) Petersfield to Guildford | O | 26 |

N.B. Type N was the new type of brake van while Type O was the old type van. A third type of brake van known as the 15 ton van was also in use. The braking power of the latter van was stated to be equal to the heavier N and O type vans.

During the years described in this book every station on the line, apart from halts, had goods sidings. Motor spirit, paraffin, farm animals, timber, grain, lime, fertilizer, machinery of all kinds, chemicals, coal and coke were transported by rail. Every station had a local coal merchant. Consequently, goods trains travelled up and down the line at all hours. On Saturdays, however, particularly in the summer, the number of goods trains was restricted during the daylight hours.

The goods trains between Woking and Portsmouth were invariably handled by Adams 0–6–0s or 0–4–2s in the case of the lighter trains. Drummond 0–6–0s of the 700 class would handle the heavier trains. The short-haul trains, Guildford to Godalming or Guildford to Woking, were almost exclusively taken by Adams 0–4–2s unless the train was very heavy or very long when a 700 class would take the train.

The N class 2–6–0s of Maunsell's design were fairly new in 1926 and did not appear on the Portsmouth line at the time the U class started to arrive. Needless to say, the N class would have been very suitable for the heavier goods trains. The N1 class would have handled the longer distance heavier goods trains ideally but one must remember that the newly constructed U1s had only just started work on this line in mid-1931 and were not yet fully proven engines. Subsequently, of course, they proved excellent replacements for the then ageing D15s. As an aside, in 1948 or 1949 I saw a rather run down U1 shunting goods wagon at Otford, Kent. It may have been due for a refit at Ashford Works but it seemed a big comedown for a locomotive that had been on semi-fast and express passenger work seventeen or eighteen years previously on the Portsmouth line. It was surprising that such a comparatively heavy engine with a fairly long fixed wheelbase could have negotiated the sharply curved sidings of Otford station without difficulty but evidently the crew managed all right.

At the start of this chapter I mentioned that a goods train in 1927 looked very different from a freight train of today. Our 1927 goods train had a goods brake van at the rear but that was by no means the only difference. Not only were there very many more goods trains operating in the twenties and thirties but the wagons and vans were smaller, apart from the odd bogie wagon, and most of the train consisted of private owner wagons. The coal merchants and colliery wagons were by far the most numerous of the private owner wagons. Many such vehicles were painted in bright colours. Some of the wagons which were painted grey or black had red or white lettering and bore the name and home town of the firm concerned. A bright, clean wagon was clearly a good travelling advertisement for a firm. A long train of sixty wagons, long for the Southern, often contained forty or fifty privately owned wagons and possibly three or four petrol tank wagons marshalled at the rear of the train immediately in front of the brake van. The tanker wagons were always kept very clean and in excellent order, they had to be so, and were the most colourful part of a goods train. Some of the old petrol companies such as Pratts, Redline and Power had brightly coloured tankers. Shell, National Benzole and Esso of the present-day companies always had vividly painted tanker wagons. A fully reconditioned and repainted Esso tank wagon was presented by that company some years ago to the Kent & East Sussex Railway. The vehicle was kept at Tenterden Town station and was a fine example of the type of tank wagon used on all the railways 50 or 60 years ago.

There were still a few pre-grouping wagons in use carrying the old railway companies' initials in 1926. This was over three years since the grouping on 1 January 1923. Those I remember on the Portsmouth line were the odd 10 or 12 ton open wagons lettered 'GC', 'GN' and 'MR'.

Wagons and vans for every kind of goods and merchandise were provided by all the railway companies, even the Southern Railway. The largest vehicles were 40 or 50 ton bogie brick wagons, bolster wagons for transporting tree trunks or telegraph poles and bogie well wagons to carry really heavy, yet comparatively compact, machinery such as boilers or electricity generators. Vans for cattle, sheep or pigs, closed general goods vans, tar wagons, gunpowder vans, small four-wheeled timber or bolster wagons and tankers were all available. There were fitted vacuum braked vans for meat, fish, fruit, ice and perishable goods. Tankers for milk are still in use of course. The list was tremendous. Finally, and quite literally, at the end of the train was the goods brake van with its coal fired stove for the guard, very necessary in winter and on a freezing winter morning at 3.00 a.m. The old South Eastern & Chatham Railway had a number of bogie brake vans which were most impressive vehicles. I can remember that they were used on ballast trains. On very rare occasions I saw one of these bogie brakes passing through Guildford on the Redhill to Reading line.

The small yellow letter which appeared on each edge of the buffer beam of ex-LSWR

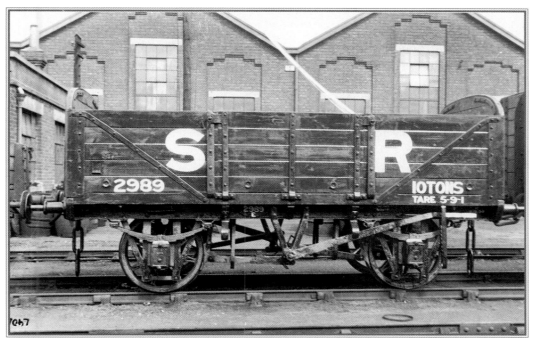

77    Southern Railway 10-ton open wagon No. 2989

78    Southern Railway 25-ton brake van No. 55964

and SR (Western Section) engines built at Eastleigh indicated the locomotive power-cum-braking capability. The working timetables listed the permitted maximum goods trains load by section, by route and for each class of locomotive. This information was needed because loads were taken on according to wagons ready for forwarding, trains being made up by yard foremen. Thus, arguments with drivers about being overloaded were obviated. Reference to Appendix IV, column 6, shows the letters allocated to the various locomotive classes indicating power/braking group. All tank engines were covered by letter K except the big Urie 4–6–2Ts and 4–8–0Ts which were classified A.

*Chapter Six*

# TIMETABLES AND PASSENGER TRAIN RUNNING

S ixty years ago or more, the number of passengers carried by train was generally far in excess of those travelling by rail today. Although the motor omnibus, motor coach, private car and motor cycle were beginning to affect rail traffic adversely, train travel was normal for most folk. Moreover, for journeys over 25 miles the steam train was faster, more comfortable and certainly much warmer in winter. Timekeeping by the railways was far superior to that of the motor omnibuses and coaches. The Portsmouth Direct line maintained a high standard of timekeeping. Some criticism, though, may be made of the summer Saturday delays at the approaches to Portsmouth. The reasons for these delays are explained later in this chapter.

On the Southern Railway, for third-class passengers up to 100 lb of luggage travelled free of charge while emigrants were allowed 112 lb free of charge. Merchant seamen were privileged for they got away with 168 lb free of charge. For commercial travellers holding first-class tickets, personal luggage and business effects up to 336 lb were allowed free of charge. The third-class limit on emigrants – immigrants were not mentioned – of 168 lb seemed a bit unfair. I would have thought they could have been dealt with on the same terms as commercial travellers. Many of these travelling representatives held season tickets covering more or less unlimited travel over huge areas. The motor car was used to a certain extent, particularly over limited areas by travellers doing their rounds, but it was not used to the extent that it is these days. During the late twenties, therefore, one can only assume that travellers on business were a good source of revenue to the railways.

Every station, however small, had a porter available to assist passengers with bulky luggage. At the terminal stations in London, the number of porters available was positively embarrassing. Trollies for the use of passengers were unheard of. A long trip by train, perhaps involving a journey from the Isle of Wight to Waterloo with a change at Portsmouth Harbour as well as at Ryde Pierhead, was no problem for an elderly person with a mountain of luggage 60 years ago or more.

Reference to the description of passengers under the appropriate regulations makes amusing reading. Apparently, luggage excluding personal luggage was limited to 60 lb per person for hucksters, packmen, travelling drapers, butchers, farmers, fishmongers and market traders among others. The limit of 60 lb also applied to workmen carrying tools and to outworkers travelling to their warehouses with goods worked on at home. Members of theatrical companies, strolling players, music hall artists and equestrian performers were allowed 168 lb of luggage free of charge if holding third-class tickets.

The service provided on the Waterloo to Portsmouth direct line during the twenties and thirties was amazingly good. In particular, the intermediate stations between Woking and Portsmouth, all fourteen of them, were served well bearing in mind that some stations such as Worplesdon, Guildford, Farncombe, Godalming and Haslemere were commuter stations for London and others such as Milford, Witley, Liphook, Liss and Rowlands Castle were country stations. Petersfield was rather different. It was a country station, yet people travelled to Portsmouth for employment, and it was also a junction for the Midhurst branch. A number of people travelled daily to London from Petersfield.

The Southern Railway timetable for 1927 shows the summer period service operated from 10 July until 25 September, and the winter service from 26 September until further notice. The general pattern for the winter service was:

1.  Stopping trains from Waterloo, semi-fast to Woking, terminating at Guildford, Haslemere or Petersfield.
2.  Semi-fast trains from Waterloo to Haslemere or Petersfield then calling at all stations to Portsmouth & Southsea or Portsmouth Harbour.
3.  Express trains non-stop Waterloo to Portsmouth.
4.  Semi-fast trains Waterloo to Portsmouth.
5.  Short-distance local stopping trains, e.g. Woking to Farncombe, Petersfield to Portsmouth, Milford to Woking, etc.

There were similar return workings.

**79**  U class 2–6–0 No. A624 working hard on the ascent to Haslemere with an express for Portsmouth Harbour (1939)

**80**  T9 4–4–0 No. E337 with a stopping train for Portsmouth & Southsea makes an easy ascent at the same
location as photograph 81. Note set of four non-corridor coaches

There was also the well-known Margate to Birkenhead train, with through carriages
for Bournemouth, which arrived at Guildford from Redhill at 12.14 p.m. The
Bournemouth carriages were attached to a Waterloo to Bournemouth via Guildford and
Fareham train at Guildford. It left at 12.33 p.m. to call at Godalming 12.42 p.m.,
Haslemere at 1.2 p.m. and Petersfield at 1.19 p.m. which it left at 1.21 p.m. to pass off
the Portsmouth line at Farlington Junction. I travelled from Deal by this train on several
occasions as far as Haslemere. It left Deal at 9.6 a.m. This interesting working entailed
reversals at Dover Marine and Redhill as well as detaching coaches at Guildford for the
Bournemouth train which left Guildford in the opposite direction. Engines were
changed at Dover Marine and at Redhill. This train popularly known as the 'Birkenhead
Express' was in truth a semi-fast and for a cross-country journey made extremely good
time. It ran thrice weekly in each direction during the winter but daily in each direction
during the summer service period. The timetable advertised it as a corridor train. Motive
power from Margate to Dover Marine station was an ex-SE&CR 4–4–0 of the D1 or E1
class. From Dover Marine to Redhill a U class 2–6–0 would take over. With the second
reversal at Redhill another U class would take the train forward to Guildford and on to
Reading (GWR).

The Up journey of the 'Birkenhead Express' over the Southern Railway as far as Redhill was:

| | |
|---|---|
| Depart Reading (GWR) | 1.10 p.m. to SR metals. |
| Arrive Guildford | 1.49 p.m. |
| Depart Guildford | 1.59 p.m. |
| Arrive Redhill | 2.30 p.m. |

A train from Bournemouth West leaving there at 10.30 a.m. would join the Portsmouth Direct line at Farlington Junction calling at Havant at 12.30 p.m., Petersfield, Liss, Haslemere and Godalming arriving at Guildford by 1.49 p.m. There, the through coaches for Margate, via Redhill, would be attached to the train from Reading ready to leave for Redhill by 1.59 p.m. The train from Bournemouth got away by 2.7 p.m. terminating at Woking at 2.20 p.m. This transfer of coaches from one train to another was certainly a feature of train handling at Guildford, hence the need for a station pilot.

Looking at the timetable more closely reminds me that certain trains on the Woking to Portsmouth run were nearly always hauled by a specific class of engine. One must remember that in 1926 the grouping had only been effective for just over three years and the Southern Railway had inherited a vast collection of steam locomotives belonging to numerous classes. Many of the classes contained only a few engines and no great programme of scrapping had taken place. A lot of engines had years of useful service left and there was no pressing need to withdraw them. To the amateur observer it appeared that each train during the day had a specific class of engine allocated to it for there was seldom any wide variation in the type of engine allocated. Consequently, any change in motive power, however minor, was quickly noticed. For instance, the 6.30 a.m. Waterloo to Portsmouth Harbour train which was semi-fast to Woking, calling at Surbiton and Weybridge, then after Woking stopping at all stations to Portsmouth Harbour was invariably a U class 2–6–0 turn. Before the Moguls arrived on the scene in 1927, a Drummond L12 4–4–0 took the train. I do remember seeing an Adams A12 0–4–2 on this train but I suspect it may have come on at Guildford, which had a large collection of these engines at the time.

The slow trains from Waterloo or Guildford which terminated at Haslemere were always headed by Drummond M7 0–4–4 tanks. Haslemere had no turntable so the use of these tank engines was fairly obvious. Upon arrival at Haslemere, after passengers had alighted, the train would draw forward from the Down platform (see track layout plan Appendix I) and then propel the train across to Platform 3 (Up). The engine would then run round the train via Platform 2, when convenient, ready for return to Guildford, Woking or Waterloo. An example was the 8.25 a.m. Saturday train from Woking which arrived at Haslemere at 9.16 a.m. This train returned from Haslemere at 10.10 a.m. eventually reaching Waterloo by 11.57 a.m., being slow to Surbiton then fast to Waterloo. A picture of one of these trains at Haslemere headed by No. E45, one of the ubiquitous M7s, appears in photograph 75 on page 68.

The 10.44 a.m. Guildford departure to Portsmouth was an interesting working. This train started as the 9.38 a.m. from Waterloo which was fast to Woking where the train

**81**  U1 2–6–0 with a Portsmouth Harbour slow train starting the 1 in 80 climb between Witley and Haslemere (1931)

**82**  No. E774 *Sir Gaheris* 'King Arthur' class with a Down train climbing towards Haslemere

was divided. The first half went on fast to Guildford leaving Woking at 10.12 a.m. and reaching Guildford at 10.23 a.m. In the meantime, the 9.50 a.m. restaurant car express from Waterloo to Portsmouth Harbour passed the second half of the 9.38 a.m. ex-Waterloo at Woking and called at Guildford at 10.29 a.m. The second half of the 9.38 a.m. then left Woking at 10.26 a.m. arriving at Guildford at 10.42 a.m. It left Guildford at 10.44 a.m. as a slow train to Portsmouth & Southsea getting in at 12.30 p.m. Quite often, this train was taken by a Drummond T14 4–6–0 'Paddlebox', which was surprising since it was a short non-corridor train. The use of such a heavy and powerful engine seemed extravagant unless, of course, it was being worked back to Fratton shed to pick up a heavy train for Waterloo later in the day.

There were three departures from Waterloo at two-hour intervals, at 11.50 a.m., 1.50 p.m. and 3.50 p.m., all non-stop to Portsmouth & Southsea and terminating at Portsmouth Harbour. These trains were normally 'King Arthur' class N15 turns. The timing from Waterloo to Portsmouth & Southsea was 99 minutes for the 73¾ miles giving an average speed of 44.7 mph. The 11.50 a.m. and the 3.50 p.m. trains had a restaurant car in their formation. In Chapter Three I mentioned that all the 'King Arthur' N15s working on this line were fitted with eight-wheeled tenders with a water capacity of 5,000 gallons. With such a hilly route, I should think the later N15s which had 4,000 gallon six-wheeled tenders might have run dangerously low after a non-stop run to Portsmouth. Yet, surprisingly, the U and later U1 classes with six-wheeled tenders holding 4,000 gallons of water often deputized on these heavy non-stop trains, especially on summer Saturdays.

While on the subject of winter restaurant car trains, during the week, Monday to Friday, there were no less than seven such fast or semi-fast trains leaving Waterloo for Portsmouth and six trains in the Up direction.

The 7.8 a.m. from Portsmouth Harbour to Waterloo was slow to Guildford and then fast to Waterloo arriving at 9.39 a.m. The 30¾ miles from Guildford to Waterloo were scheduled for 39 minutes giving an average speed of 47.3 mph. This was an all the year round train carrying many commuters after calling at Haslemere. For many years this train was a Drummond D15 4–4–0 turn without exception. From 1926 to 1929 every one of the engines in this class, there were ten numbered from E463 to E472, appeared on the train. When the newly built U1 class left Eastleigh in 1931, the D15s gradually disappeared. This 7.8 a.m. train was invariably packed after Godalming with standing room only for the last leg from Guildford to Waterloo. Moreover, the train was always made up with non-corridor stock. The D15s put up fine performances between Haslemere and Guildford even though stops were made at all the intermediate stations. From Guildford to Waterloo speeds of up to 75 mph in places were quite common, though the approach to Waterloo was frequently subject to signal checks. The U1 Moguls which followed the D15s were 25 per cent up on tractive effort and had superior acceleration with their three cylinders and smaller driving wheels (6 ft as against 6 ft 7 in). These engines certainly transformed timekeeping on the line but one must not detract from the splendid performance of the D15s, which by 1931 were 18 years old.

The winter Sunday service was not at all good by modern standards. There were but six Down trains and only five Up trains covering the whole distance between Waterloo

**83** U 2–6–0 No. A623 with a semi-fast train for Portsmouth Harbour accelerates away from Haslemere (1931)

**84** D15 4–4–0 No. 470 on a Portsmouth to Cardiff train at Westbury (GWR)

and Portsmouth. I think this may have reflected the general attitude of people nearly 60 years ago when Sunday was more often observed as a day of rest and when many more people attended church regularly.

A feature of passenger train running on this line during the late twenties, and indeed the thirties, was the huge number of trains dealt with on summer Saturdays both at Guildford and at Fratton. For example, at Guildford an analysis shows that between 6.30 a.m. and 11.30 p.m. no less than 102 scheduled Down trains used the station. This number excludes electric trains running via Effingham Junction to and from Waterloo which used the bay platform. The total number of 102 is made up of non-stop trains en route for Portsmouth, trains calling at Guildford and those starting or terminating at Guildford. One must remember that the total includes not only trains for Portsmouth, and any terminating at stations on the way, but also the Redhill to Reading trains (Redhill to Reading was reckoned to be 'Down') as well as the Horsham branch trains and Farnham line trains. The busiest time was from 1.00 p.m. to 1.59 p.m. when eleven Down trains were dealt with. The total number of Up trains can be assumed to be about the same. If we add a few excursions, specials, empty coach trains, light engines and a few goods trains, the overall picture was certainly one of intense activity. Except through Guildford station itself there was only normal double track and, since semaphore signals were universal, the signalmen really earned their pay on a Saturday. Standing at the south-western end of what was Platform 1 in those days, it is now Platform 2, a clear view could be had right through St Catherine's tunnel providing a train had cleared the tunnel by at least five minutes. Very often though, dense clouds of steam and smoke belching from the tunnel made a clear through sighting quite impossible. (The present numbering of platforms is from 1 to 8 since the old No. 1 Bay became Platform 1 and all other platforms had 1 added to their original number.)

Fratton station too was very busy on summer Saturdays for the same reasons that applied to Guildford. The running sheds, roundhouse and turntable at Fratton were extensive and not nearly so cramped as at Guildford. Furthermore, Central Section trains from Victoria, Brighton and the South Coast, as well as trains from Waterloo, passed through or called on their way to Portsmouth. In addition, trains from Southampton, Eastleigh and Salisbury joined the main Portsmouth line at Portcreek Junction just before reaching Fratton. A number of long-distance trains from such places as Bristol, Cardiff, York and Birmingham also passed through to Portsmouth. From 6.24 a.m. to 2.17 a.m. next day, ninety-seven Down passenger trains were handled at Fratton on a summer Saturday. I think it probable that more light engines passed through Fratton for coaling, watering and turning than at Guildford. There were no such facilities either at Portsmouth Harbour or Portsmouth & Southsea though a small turntable was installed at Burnaby Road between the two Portsmouth stations. Even so, the longest engines, such as the 'King Arthurs', the odd 'Lord Nelson' or a Drummond T9 4–4–0 with eight-wheeled tender, had to use the Fratton triangle for turning. On balance, therefore, I would think that Fratton was a busier station than Guildford as regards train and locomotive movements. There was only one Down running line beyond Fratton for passenger trains to both the Portsmouth stations so one can understand why many trains were allowed up to ten minutes extra time on summer Saturdays from Havant to

**85**  Rebuilt D1 4–4–0 No. 502 (later A502) in SE&CR finish. Note three-coach 'Birdcage' set next to engine (1922)

**86**  N15 class 4–6–0 No. E748 *Vivien* on Down Portsmouth Harbour train, near Esher

**87** N15 class 4–6–0 No. E747 *Elaine* at Witley with a Down slow train to Portsmouth Harbour (1937)

Portsmouth Harbour. At Havant, and at all signal-boxes to the end of the line, a signalman's life must have been very hard in those days.

I think it might give the reader an even better idea of how congested the line was for the last eight miles to Portsmouth Harbour, especially on a summer Saturday, if I now list the signal-boxes that were in operation in steam days, at least up to 1931. The names of the signal-boxes were:

Havant Junction (66½ miles from Waterloo)
Havant West
Bedhampton Mill (reduced to ground frame 17.4.29)
Farlington Intermediate (closed 22.8.29)
Farlington Junction
Port Creek Junction
Green Lanes Crossing

Copnor
Fratton East
Fratton West
Portsmouth East
Portsmouth Yard
Portsmouth High Level
Burnaby Road
Portsmouth Harbour (74½ miles from Waterloo)

With fifteen signal-boxes in the eight miles concerned, or say one box every half mile, and up to June 1937 only one Down passenger line, severe congestion was unavoidable. Even so, there were still more problems for the signalmen to contend with on summer Saturdays. During the summer months, many big companies with factories in the North,

88   N15 4–6–0 No. 746 *Pendragon* at Petersfield with a slow train to Portsmouth & Southsea (1937)

**89** 'Schools' class 4–4–0 No. 933 *King's Canterbury* on Up Waterloo train at Liphook (1937)

as well as in the north and south Midlands, chartered special trains on summer Saturdays for their workers' annual holidays. The Isle of Wight and Southsea were favourite destinations. I was told by a railwayman, once a signalman, who is a member of an old railway family, that Dunlop Tyres from Birmingham, Black Cat Cigarettes and Morris Motors of Cowley, Oxford were some of the companies making use of special trains. The engine carried a headboard bearing the name of the company chartering the train. Most of these trains would enter the Portsmouth area through Cosham, Cosham Junction and Port Creek Junction (see track layouts in Appendix I). Nearly all trains were brought to a dead stop at each box from Cosham onwards. Sometimes a train would stand for five, ten or even fifteen minutes at a time. Looking back, it seems incredible that a second Down passenger line from Fratton was not introduced until 1937. An examination of the track layout between Fratton and Portsmouth shows an extra Down line was available but this appeared to serve the Greetham Street goods sidings (closed in 1936) adjacent to Portsmouth & Southsea station.

The engine disc or lamp headcodes indicating the route were as follows between 1923 and 1933:

### Waterloo to Portsmouth & Southsea

Three discs or lamps if the train was partially or fully travelling during the hours of darkness. One disc was placed in front of the chimney and one disc each side of the smokebox. Examples appear in photographs 69 and 80.

### Waterloo to Portsmouth Harbour

Three discs or lamps, one over each buffer and one on the left-hand side of the smokebox when facing the engine. Photographs 30, 81, 82 and 83 indicate this variation.

### Up trains to Waterloo

Three discs or lamps, one in front of the chimney, one on the right-hand side of the smokebox and one over the left-hand buffer when facing the engine. Photograph 20 is a clear example.

All these headcodes, along with other three-disc codes, were revised in 1934 in order to rationalize the practice of the three constituent companies. Moreover, two-disc headcodes reduced the number of discs or lamps in use, a good point in all respects. It was also unnecessary to have differing codes for Up and Down trains between Portsmouth and Waterloo.

Although electric operation of the line commenced on 4 July 1937, steam trains continued to use the line. These were goods, van trains, excursions, certain cross-country trains and special trains. Some of these trains continued to use three-disc headcodes. Photographs 73, 87, 88, 89, 91 and 92 show the revised two-disc headcodes used from 1934 onwards. Photograph 88 shows the code for trains starting or terminating at Portsmouth & Southsea while 73, 87, 89, 91 and 92 show the corresponding code for Portsmouth Harbour trains.

The Southern Railway always had an excellent record for safety and freedom from serious accidents. This was particularly so on the Portsmouth Direct line. Between 1926 and 1937 there were no major accidents and only one member of the public travelling by train as a passenger between Woking and Portsmouth lost his life.

A scrutiny of the Board of Trade Accident Reports 1926–37 shows there were eight accidents involving serious injury to staff on duty. Loss of life resulted in four cases. At Woking, a foreman ganger was unfortunately struck down and killed in August 1936 by a train passing Woking at speed. In spite of heavy application of the brakes and repeated whistling he did not appear to hear the train approaching. On 28 October 1936 at Guildford, an engineer working for a private contractor on the electrification of the line was fatally hit by an engine and five wagons shunting. He had left his train and taken a short cut off the platform to his home not far from the station. His line walking permit did not allow him to be on the track when off duty. About a month later, at Haslemere, a senior porter of long service to the company failed to see a light engine passing by while he was assisting in shunting operations. He was fatally injured. A combination of bad circumstances at the time was thought to be the cause. The fourth case occurred in Buriton Tunnel south of Petersfield in 1926. A member of the permanent way staff at

**90**   A12 class 0–4–2 No. E527 leaving Guildford with an Up train for Woking

**91**   'Schools' class No. 930 *Radley* with Up Waterloo train entering Portsmouth & Southsea (high-level station)

**92** Up Waterloo train waiting to start from Portsmouth Harbour station. 'Schools' class No. 932 *Blundells*

Petersfield lost his life during ballasting operations in the tunnel. He was knocked down by a wagon while the train was backing slowly in order to discharge ballast.

There were four serious accidents between 1926 and 1937 involving members of the staff while on duty, one each at Fratton Yard and Havant and two at Portsmouth & Southsea. Fortunately, none of these accidents was fatal. Again, staff involved in shunting or on permanent way work were the victims.

The conclusion one can draw from these accidents is that while many railwaymen are at great risk on duty, permanent way staff and shunting staff were the most vulnerable, closely followed by footplate crews. Staff were almost always careful and precise in their performance of duty but unfortunately the occasional lapse, allied to freak circumstances, frequently proved serious or fatal.

Before closing this chapter on passenger train running and accidents in particular, readers might be interested to hear of an early accident, actually well outside the time-

93   No. 118 steams again – piloting an Up train at Battledown Flyover on the West of England main line
(1948)

scale of this book, which took place in 1872. The cause of the accident was so unusual that I mention it here.

On 12 February 1872, the 12.21 p.m. train from Portsmouth to London hauled by a 2–4–0 engine named *Colne* struck a bullock which had strayed on to the line between Peasmarsh Junction and Shalford Junction (see gradient profile in Appendix II for precise location). The unfortunate animal was killed by the impact and fell between the tender and the first passenger coach. The six-wheeled coaches were derailed and severely damaged. A number of passengers were injured but there was no loss of life to passengers or train crew. The engine *Colne* was undamaged and driven on to Guildford in order to give the alarm.

*Chapter Seven*

# FROM ELECTRIFICATION TO WARTIME

After the official start of electrification on 4 July 1937, just 26 months lay ahead to the outbreak of war against Germany on 3 September 1939. The frequency of the passenger trains and their overall speed showed a clear advance over the steam trains. But, one had to admit that the steam trains were smoother, quieter and more comfortable than the electric multiple unit trains. The electric trains had lost the character of the steam trains and, apart from varying lengths, were all the same. The general public were impressed with the better service and revenue increased, so the directors of the Southern Railway were pleased.

Goods trains remained steam hauled on the Portsmouth Direct line as did certain cross-country passenger and goods trains, and van or parcels trains. At Guildford, the Reading to Redhill line and the Guildford to Horsham line kept steam alive. There were some changes in locomotive power and the number of locomotives stabled both at Guildford and Fratton declined. The ten 'Schools' class engines at Fratton were moved to other lines.

There were also a number of track layout alterations, mainly at Portsmouth & Southsea where the Greetham Street Goods station was closed and the work transferred to Fratton. The Down siding from Fratton to Greetham Street Goods was at long last converted to an additional Down relief line. Berthing sidings at Fratton and Portsmouth & Southsea were installed for the multiple unit electric trains.

In the early part of 1939, plans for the evacuation of the elderly and children were drawn up by the government. The first job of any size for the railway companies was the running of special trains. The Southern Railway ran many special trains carrying evacuees to evacuation areas on or near the Portsmouth Direct line. When war was declared on 3 September 1939, the full impact of evacuation took place. By then the four main railway companies were under government control. This control was delegated to the Railway Executive Committee based in London. Numerous measures then applied, to the Southern Railway in particular and to the railways in general. Journey times were increased and a speed limit of 60 mph was introduced.

*Chapter Eight*

# WARTIME

T he Portsmouth Direct line now virtually lost its individuality and became no more than a minor part of the Southern Railway which in itself now formed part of one huge railway system. This system covered the whole of the British Isles except Eire, which was neutral. Control passed to the government which in turn delegated the day-to-day running and general administration to the Railway Executive based in London. The government controlled the financial side and allocated an agreed portion of the total receipts to each of the four main line companies.

From 1 September 1939, the 60 mph speed limit involved a reduction in services and some drastic increases in journey times. Evacuation of children and the elderly from danger areas had started on 31 August 1939. Portsmouth and Gosport was one danger area where such evacuation had already taken place. Blackout arrangements at stations, marshalling yards, engine sheds and in trains, and other air raid precautions saddled the railways with an enormous amount of extra work. The Southern Railway was affected more than any of the other companies since it was nearest enemy territory. However, the 60 mph speed limit in itself did not unduly trouble the SR because it had no really long-distance runs such as the other railways, e.g. to Scotland, to Wales or to the extreme west of England.

The government expected air raids on the Portsmouth and Southampton areas for certain, mainly because Portsmouth was a naval town and Southampton had extensive docks and the enemy would regard both places as legitimate targets. From 1940 right up to late 1944, Portsmouth and Southampton suffered from enemy air attacks.

Many subsidiary facilities such as weekend and cheap day tickets, holiday runabout tickets, reserved seats and restaurant cars had to be withdrawn. Excursion trains were also withdrawn. The general effect of all these wartime restrictions was to concentrate more passengers into fewer trains which occupied longer journey times. Travelling under blackout conditions late at night was difficult in many ways not only for passengers but also for the train crews.

Turning now to the effect on goods traffic, the first item of real importance was the absorption of all private owners' goods wagons into the common pool of railway companies' wagons. This in effect did away with the work of the Railway Clearing House almost completely. On the Southern Railway as a whole and on the Portsmouth line in particular, there was a strong build-up of goods traffic. While the armed services were mainly responsible, there was nevertheless a considerable build-up in the transport of manufactured goods and fuel, all of which needed railway transport. The Southern Railway, being predominately a passenger carrying line, was affected more than the other three companies by this rise in goods traffic. One side effect of this increase was the need for extra locomotives. With the decrease in the number of steam-hauled passenger trains, many of the N15 'King Arthur' class 4–6–0s became available. Some of these engines worked in and out of Fratton with goods trains.

The next event which affected the Southern Railway directly was the evacuation of troops from Dunkirk in June 1940. Over several days 330,000 troops were landed at various ports on the south-east and south coasts. Although the Portsmouth line was only indirectly affected, many of the trains ferrying troops away from the ports to dispersal centres passed through Guildford and on to Reading, where they were taken over by the Great Western Railway. Passenger coaches and locomotives of all types, except tank engines, were urgently required at the landing ports on the coast. Some of these ports were Dover, Folkestone, Newhaven, Ramsgate, Sheerness, Margate and Southampton. Most older people will remember that the Dunkirk evacuation was a brilliant operation carried out by all concerned. The railways, in particular, performed a most difficult task in an exemplary manner. I happened to be staying at Rochester, Kent, at the time of the Dunkirk operation, quite close to the railway bridge over the River Medway. One fine June morning in 1940 I was puzzled by the number of steam trains travelling towards London. There seemed to be one every 5 or 10 minutes and they went on and on. Then I saw there were soldiers leaning out of the windows. The general public knew nothing of this. All we had been told was that the Allies had fallen back towards Dunkirk. There was no word of an evacuation. Many of these trains were of four or five coaches from the LMS or the LNER as well as the usual SR stock. The engines I saw were all from the SR. By this time the news was out and we knew it all. From June 1940, the enemy forces lined the Channel coast on the French, Belgian and Dutch sides. Consequently, the Southern Railway expected air raids, shelling and invading troops either by sea or as parachutists. The Dover to Deal line of the SR was but 21 miles from the enemy-held coast. Portsmouth was further from the enemy coast but close enough to be uncomfortable. There was great activity all along the coast from Margate to Weymouth which went on from June 1940 until early in 1941. We all knew that the enemy retired baffled, frustrated and beaten, for the moment.

In January 1941, there was an air raid in the Portsmouth and Southampton area. Among other damage in the area, the enemy had scored a direct hit on Fratton engine shed. One of the T9s, No. 118, received a bomb through the firebox which upended the tender and damaged the engine but not severely. This was not the end for No. 118; Drummond engines were tough and she was deemed worth repairing. The engine was taken to Eastleigh, fitted with a new boiler and firebox, and other repairs were carried out. The engine returned to service (see photograph 93 on page 96 taken about 1948).

In May 1941, another air raid on Portsmouth wrecked a signal-box and severely damaged an electric multiple unit train which had to be broken up on the spot. From May 1941 to June 1944 enemy air attacks on the Portsmouth area eased considerably, but there were repercussions following constant air raids in and around Waterloo station which affected the Portsmouth line among others.

An interesting experiment took place in July 1941 when one of the H16 class 4–6–2 tank engines hauled an express passenger train from Waterloo to Portsmouth. The trip was apparently completed satisfactorily. This trial may have been undertaken to see if a large tank engine could do the job in case of a big electricity power failure. I would think that a water stop at Guildford would have been essential as these engines had only a 2,000 gallon tank capacity. With a 3½ ton capacity coal bunker, there would have been ample coal for 74 miles.

During the build-up for the June 1944 invasion force for France, the electric train services were reduced by 60 per cent during non-business hours. This equated to an overall reduction of 30 per cent as compared with the pre-war winter services. The period concerned was from January to June 1944. In November and December 1944, the Southampton and Portsmouth area was targeted by V1 Flying Bombs. Some damage was inflicted on Portsmouth Harbour station but this was the last time that an attack was made on Portsmouth.

Records show that, surprisingly, the Portsmouth Harbour to Ryde Pierhead steamer service, which carried over a million passengers per annum pre-war, had functioned all through the war years. There were delays and cancellations but nevertheless a service was maintained. I remember travelling from Waterloo to Ventnor in December 1945 when the journey was almost up to pre-war electric standards. After a calm and pleasant steamer journey to Ryde, it was a real pleasure to join the steam train to Ventnor. The engine and train were just as I had remembered them from pre-war days. The recovery on the Southern Railway, considering the war with Japan had ended only four months previously, was remarkable.

Finally, to finish off the wartime years, I should now like to list some additional data on locomotives and train running on or partly on the Portsmouth line during the war years:

1.  In January 1942 a through service from Ashford, Kent, to Newcastle-on-Tyne was introduced mainly for the benefit of troops going on or returning from leave. This train joined the Portsmouth line at Shalford Junction and left it immediately after the Guildford stop. At first, it was made up with LNER coaches. SR U or N class 2–6–0s handed over at Banbury to LNER engines.

2.  By April 1943 these through trains were made up with SR stock northbound on Mondays, Wednesdays and Fridays.

3.  In April 1944 the 60 mph speed limit was raised to 70 mph.

4.  Between 5 and 19 May 1945, a two-week celebration was held at Guildford to mark the centenary of the opening of the Woking to Guildford railway on 5 May 1845.

5.  In April 1945, No. 458 0–4–0 ST *Ironside* returned from Stewarts Lane shed via Redhill. This little engine had been stationed at Guildford between 1926 and 1939. It was still there at the end of the SR on 31 December 1947.

By 8 May 1945, the war with Germany was over, though from early in March 1945 it was clear that the end was near. Railway blackouts had been relaxed and services were gradually restored to pre-war levels. The very heavy goods traffic had subsided and passenger traffic, while heavy, had passed its peak.

By August 1945 the Japanese had surrendered and the railways were hoping to return to normal. Before normality, though, there were arrears of maintenance to be done on locomotives, rolling stock, track, signalling, buildings and equipment. Experienced staff at most levels were short and much training had to be put in hand. It needed at least two or three years and much expenditure to return to pre-war levels. But nationalization was on the cards. The Southern Railway had barely 2½ years to exist before it was swallowed up by British Railways.

# THE LAST YEARS OF THE SOUTHERN RAILWAY

So far as the Portsmouth Direct line was concerned, the wartime restrictions gradually eased, in common with the whole railway system, from the end of the war with Germany early in May 1945. This easing process had started very gradually in 1944 with the raising of the speed limit to 70 mph and the cessation of blackout regulations. The Southern Railway made a very quick recovery from wartime austerity and by 1946 services were returning rapidly to peacetime levels. A severe winter in 1946/7, coupled with a coal shortage, did not help but the Southern Railway staff rose to the occasion. As an aside, I remember travelling daily by electric train from Otford in Kent to Holborn Viaduct during a long spell of heavy snowfalls and icy conditions. We were stuck in a four-coach electric train at Otford. The conductor rail was iced up and a deep drift of snow forced the train to a standstill. We waited for nearly half an hour. Then, a C class Wainwright 0–6–0 from Tonbridge came along the Down line, crossed to the Up line and backed slowly on to the marooned electric train. We were ignominiously hauled smartly to Swanley Junction.

Returning now to the Portsmouth line, the goods services remained steam hauled, mainly by Adams 0–6–0s and A12 0–4–2s with 700 class 0–6–0s taking the heavier trains. Apart from minor alterations, the goods sidings operated as in pre-war days. Fratton, of course, handled the goods trains formerly dealt with at Portsmouth Greetham Street yard, which had been transformed into an electric train berthing area in 1937.

In 1947 HM King George VI and Queen Elizabeth with Princess Elizabeth and Princess Margaret set off for a 3½ month royal tour of South Africa. They left Waterloo in the Royal Train on 31 January. Appropriately, locomotive No. 850 *Lord Nelson* hauled the train to Portsmouth Harbour station. The arrangements went according to plan much to the relief of all concerned. The return journey was scheduled for 12 May 1947, so the SR powers that be decided to leave the final arrangements until a few days beforehand. It is a well-known fact that trouble arrives when least expected and so it happened when arrangements for the return journey were put in hand.

I would like to conclude with the reminiscence an old friend of mine, Bill Bishop. He has long since retired having served the Southern Railway and British Railways for 51 years. His father spent 33 years on the London & South Western Railway while Bill's grandfather spent 50 years with the same company. That was not all, for Bill's great grandfather served 30 years on the LSWR starting in 1854. What a wonderful record, 164 years in one family.

## A HOT JOB

### *by Bill Bishop*

I was a boilersmith at Eastleigh Locomotive Running Shed. During May 1947 I was sent on loan to Fratton Locomotive Running Shed when both of their boilersmiths were away. I was no stranger to Fratton as I had spent three years of my apprenticeship there. On Monday 12 May King George VI and Queen Elizabeth were to travel by the Royal Train from Portsmouth to London.

During Saturday morning 10 May, locomotive No. 850 *Lord Nelson* arrived in Fratton yard to take the Royal Train to London the following Monday. It was followed by another 'Lord Nelson' locomotive to cover it in any emergency. The fire was thrown out of both locomotives and I was instructed to examine them as to their condition. Knowing Nine Elms was their home depot I did not expect to find them in a first-class condition. I was not surprised. When I got into the fireboxes I found the tube plates covered with water leaking from tubes. I told the foreman I did not think either engine was fit for service on any train, let alone the Royal Train. The foreman informed the Chief Boiler Inspector at Brighton and the District Inspector at Eastleigh. Both men arrived in a short time. I had certainly put the cat among the pigeons that morning.

**94**  No. 850 *Lord Nelson* in Fratton locomotive yard, 11 May 1947. Bill Bishop and mate standing on the tender during a break to cool down. From left to right: Bill Clayton, chargehand fitter, Dick Everett, locomotive foreman in bowler hat, then ten cleaners, a driver and on the far right one of the running shed foremen

After examining the locomotives the inspectors suggested I work on No. 850 and two semi-skilled tubers on the stand-by engine. The next morning, Sunday, I signed on at Eastleigh and collected my acetylene carbide lamp as I knew the engines were too long to be turned into any of the shed roads and Fratton did not have any electric lead extension long enough to reach them in the yard. I was better off with my carbide lamp than the tubers who had only paraffin oil lamps which gave out plenty of smoke. However, we all had to work under the same bad conditions. The locomotives were still very hot and they could not be cooled down. The tubers were lucky as there were two of them and they took it in turn to expand a few tubes and then changed places. I had to work on my own as my mate was not paid the semi-skilled rate to repair tubes. I could only work in the firebox for fifteen minutes and then had to come out and cool down. During one of these breaks the photo of No. 850 was taken. It was a long hot job for all of us. The tubers were well in front of me but during the afternoon they were called away on a derailment which gave me a chance to complete my locomotive and return to Eastleigh to sign off at 8.00 p.m. The tubers also signed off at 8.00 p.m. as they had to complete their repairs after returning from the derailment.

Next morning, Monday, we were in the yard, not I may say to wave to the king, but to make sure *Lord Nelson* cleared our area. Things must have gone as planned as we did not have any reports to answer for any lost time. We expected to be thanked by Head Office for making the locomotives serviceable under such bad working conditions but were not advised. I expect they said we were well rewarded by being paid fourteen hours at double-time rate. The cleaners also had to be paid extra as they normally never worked on Sundays. Those two engines cost Fratton quite a tidy sum in wages just to take one train out. Nine Elms must have been surprised to find two of their engines in such a good condition.

*Appendix I*

# STATION TRACK PLANS

## Portsmouth Harbour (1900 – 1936)

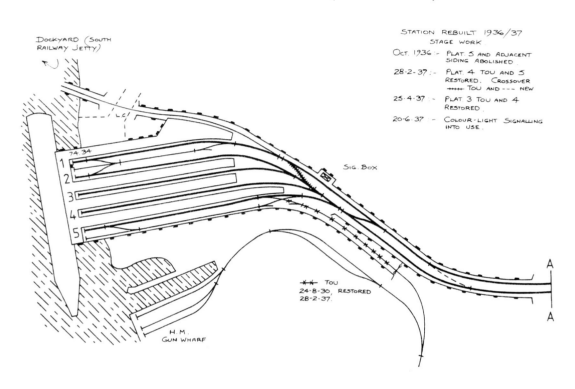

STATION REBUILT 1936/37
STAGE WORK

OCT. 1936 :- PLAT. 5 AND ADJACENT
SIDING ABOLISHED.

28·2·37 :- PLAT. 4 TOU AND 5
RESTORED. CROSSOVER
++++ TOU AND --- NEW

25·4·37 :- PLAT. 3 TOU AND 4
RESTORED.

20·6·37 - COLOUR-LIGHT SIGNALLING
INTO USE.

DOCKYARD (SOUTH
RAILWAY JETTY)

SIG. BOX

74·34

1
2
3
4
5

H.M.
GUN WHARF

✕✕ TOU
24·8·30, RESTORED
28·2·37.

A
A

A
A

## Burnaby Road (1920)

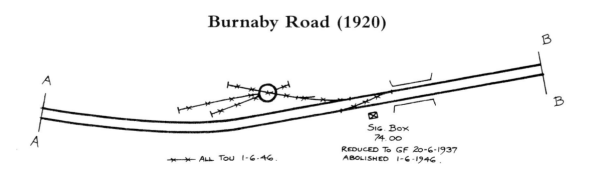

B
B

B
B

A
A

A
A

SIG. BOX
74·00

REDUCED TO GF 20·6·1937
ABOLISHED 1·6·1946.

✕—✕ ALL TOU 1·6·46.

103

# Portsmouth Town (1906)
# Portsmouth & Southsea (1921)

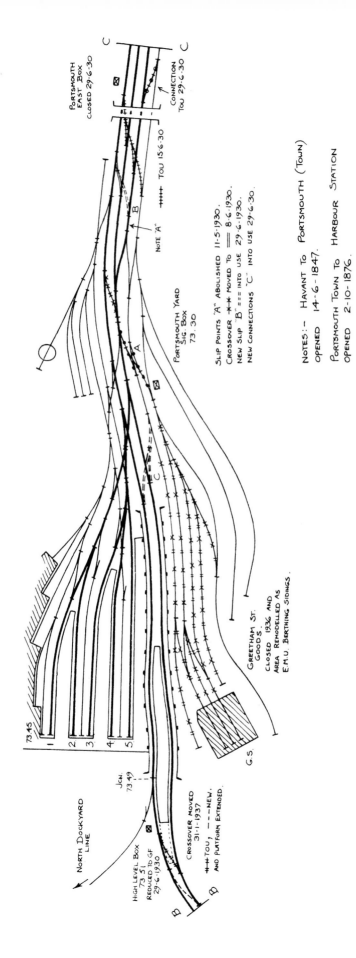

Portsmouth East Box
Closed 29-6-30

Connection Tou 29-6-30

Tou 15-6-30

+++ Tou 15-6-30

Note "A"

B

A

Portsmouth Yard Sig. Box
73.30

NOTES:— HAVANT TO PORTSMOUTH (TOWN)
OPENED 14-6-1847.

PORTSMOUTH TOWN TO HARBOUR STATION
OPENED 2-10-1876.

ELECTRIFIED (WATERLOO – PORTSMOUTH HBR.
VIA GUILDFORD) 4-7-1937.

SLIP POINTS "A" ABOLISHED 11-5-1930.
CROSSOVER ✗✗ MOVED TO ══ 8-6-1930.
NEW SLIP "B" ═══ INTO USE 29-6-1930.
NEW CONNECTIONS "C" INTO USE 29-6-30.

NOTE "A":- Nº 1 DOWN SIDING BECAME DOWN RELIEF
LINE 20-6-37.

73.45

1
2
3
4
5

C

Greetham St. Goods.
Closed 1936 and
area remodelled as
E.M.U. Berthing Sidings.

G.S.

North Dockyard Line

Jcn.
73.49

High Level Box
73.51
Reduced to GF
29-6-1930

Crossover Moved
31-1-1937.
+++ TOU; ─── NEW.
AND PLATFORM EXTENDED.

B
B

# Fratton (1900–1937)

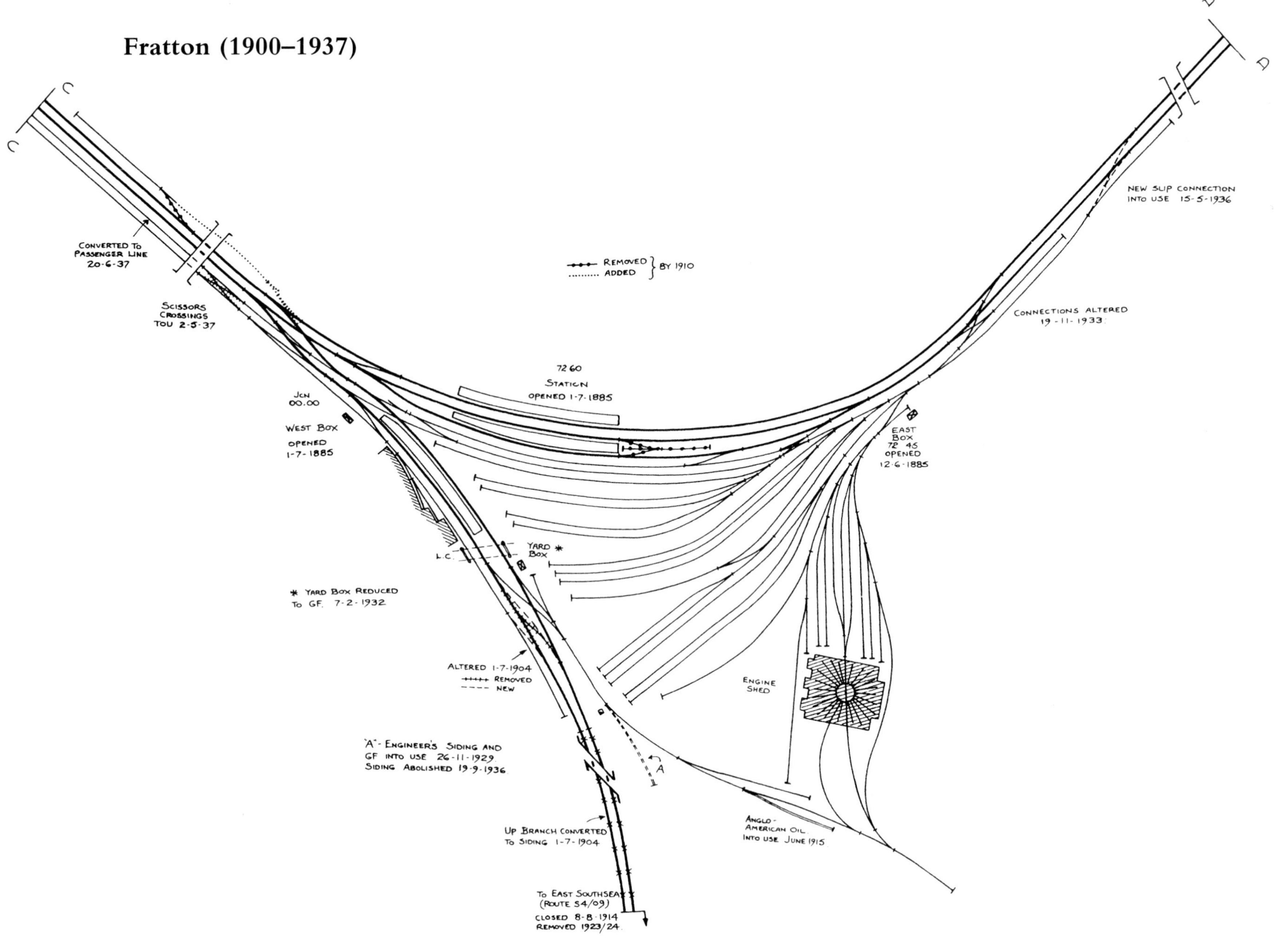

New Slip Connection into Use 15·5·1936

Connections Altered 19·11·1933

East Box 72·45 Opened 12·6·1885

Engine Shed

Anglo-American Oil into Use June 1915

Removed } By 1910
Added }

7260

Station Opened 1·7·1885

* Yard Box

Jcn. 00·00

West Box Opened 1·7·1885

Altered 1·7·1904
Removed
New

* Yard Box Reduced to GF 7·2·1932

'A'· Engineer's Siding and GF into Use 26·11·1929 Siding Abolished 19·9·1936

Up Branch Converted to Siding 1·7·1904

To East Southsea (Route 54/09) Closed 8·8·1914 Removed 1923/24

L.C.

Converted to Passenger Line 20·6·37

Scissors Crossings Tou 2·5·37

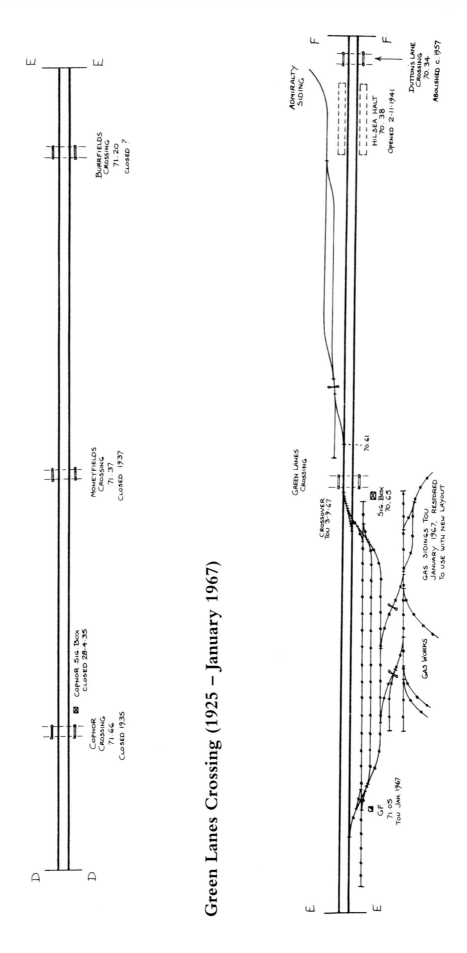

**Copnor**

**Green Lanes Crossing (1925 – January 1967)**

E

E

Burrfields
Crossing
71.20
Closed ?

Moneyfields
Crossing
71.37
Closed 1937

Copnor Sig. Box
Closed 28-4-35

Copnor
Crossing
71.66
Closed 1935

D

D

Admiralty
Siding

F

F

Hilsea Halt
70.38
Opened 2-11-1941

Duttons Lane
Crossing
70.34
Abolished c.1957

70.61

Green Lanes
Crossing

Crossover
Tou 3-9-67

Sig. Box
70.63

Gas Sidings Tou
January 1967. Restored
To use with new layout

Gas Works

GF
71.05
Tou Jan. 1967

E

E

# Farlington Triangle (1910)

# Bedhampton (1896)

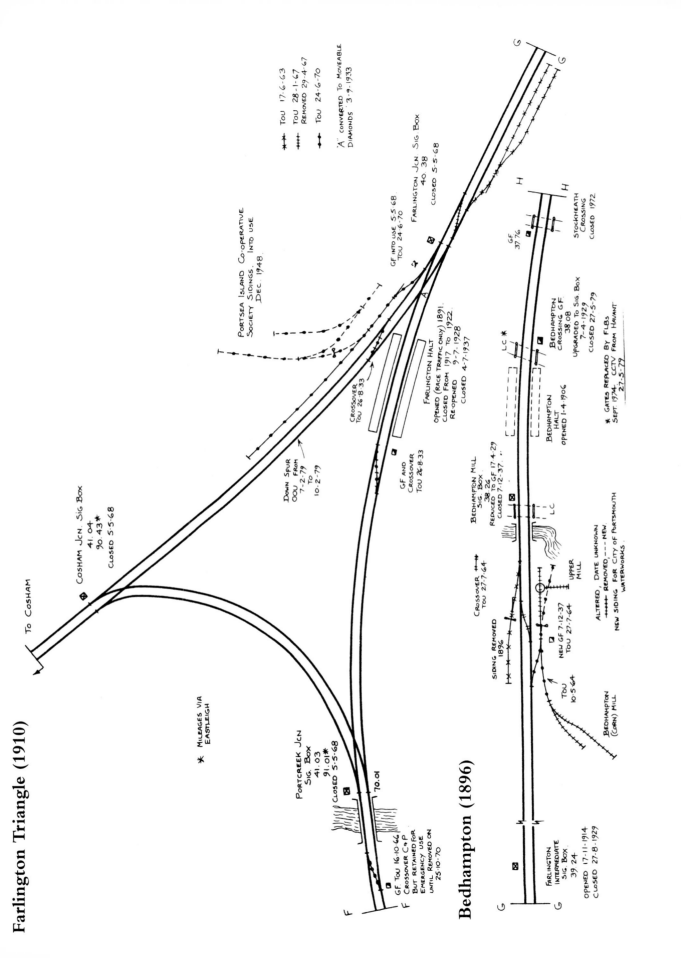

TOU 17-6-63
TOU 28-1-67
REMOVED 29-4-67
TOU 24-6-70

"A" CONVERTED TO MOVEABLE
DIAMONDS 3-9-1933

PORTSEA ISLAND CO-OPERATIVE
SOCIETY SIDINGS. INTO USE
DEC. 1948

GF INTO USE 5-5-68
TOU 24-6-70

FARLINGTON JCN SIG BOX
40.38
CLOSED 5-5-68

GF
37.76

STOCKHEATH
CROSSING
CLOSED 1972

CROSSOVER
TOU 26-8-33

DOWN SPUR
OOU FROM
7-2-79
TO
10-2-79

FARLINGTON HALT
OPENED (RACE TRAFFIC ONLY) 1891.
CLOSED FROM 1917 TO 1922.
RE-OPENED 9-7-1928
CLOSED 4-7-1937

GF AND
CROSSOVER
TOU 26-8-33

LC

BEDHAMPTON
HALT
OPENED 1-4-1906

BEDHAMPTON
CROSSING GF
38.08
UPGRADED TO SIG BOX
7-4-1929
CLOSED 27-5-79

TO COSHAM

COSHAM JCN. SIG BOX
41.04
90.43*
CLOSED 5-5-68

BEDHAMPTON MILL
SIG. BOX
38.26
REDUCED TO GF 17-4-29
CLOSED 7-12-37 "

LC

* GATES REPLACED BY FLBS
SEPT 1974, CCTV FROM HAVANT
27-5-79

* MILEAGES VIA
EASTLEIGH

CROSSOVER
TOU 27-7-64

UPPER
MILL

ALTERED, DATE UNKNOWN
——— REMOVED, --- NEW.
NEW SIDING FOR CITY OF PORTSMOUTH
WATERWORKS.

PORTCREEK JCN
SIG. BOX
41.03
91.01*
CLOSED 5-5-68

70.01

SIDING REMOVED
1896

NEW GF 7-12-37
TOU 27-7-64

TOU
10-5-64

GF TOU 16-10-66
CROSSOVER C&P
BUT RETAINED FOR
EMERGENCY USE
UNTIL REMOVED ON
25-10-70

F

BEDHAMPTON
(CORN) MILL

G

FARLINGTON
INTERMEDIATE
SIG. BOX
39.24
OPENED 17-11-1914
CLOSED 27-8-1929

G

# Havant (1920 – 1938)

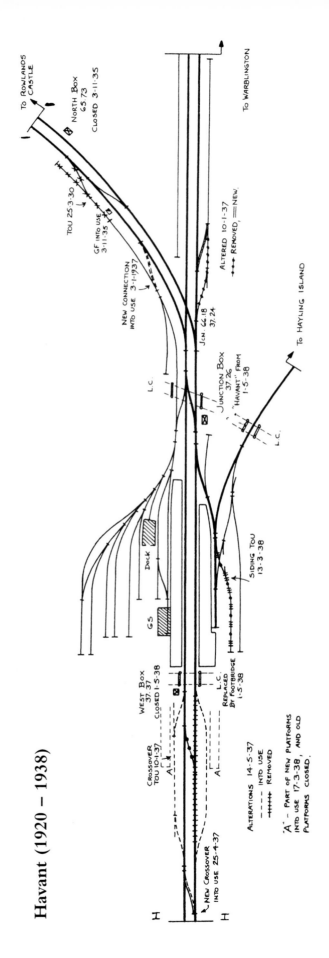

To ROWLANDS CASTLE

North Box 65.73
CLOSED 3-11-35

TOU 25-3-30

GF INTO USE 3-11-35

NEW CONNECTION INTO USE 3-1-1937

JCN. 66.18 37.24

To WARBLINGTON

ALTERED 10-1-37

REMOVED, ══════ NEW.

To HAYLING ISLAND

JUNCTION BOX 37.26 "HAVANT" FROM 1-5-38

L.C.

L.C.

Dock

GS

SIDING TOU 13-3-38

WEST BOX 37.37 CLOSED 1-5-38

L.C. REPLACED BY FOOTBRIDGE 1-5-38

CROSSOVER TOU 10-1-37

"A"

"A"

ALTERATIONS 14-5-37

────── INTO USE
++++++ REMOVED

"A" - PART OF NEW PLATFORMS INTO USE 17-3-38, AND OLD PLATFORMS CLOSED.

NEW CROSSOVER INTO USE 25-4-37

H                    H

# Rowlands Castle (1915)

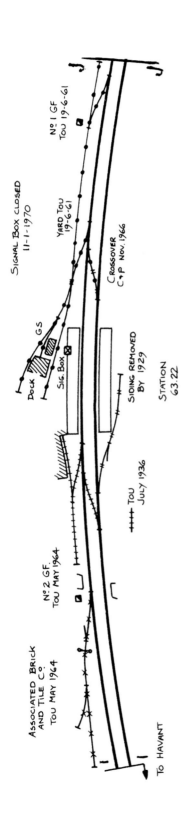

SIGNAL BOX CLOSED 11-1-1970

No 1 GF TOU 19-6-61

YARD TOU 19-6-61

CROSSOVER C+P NOV. 1966

GS

Dock

SIG. BOX

SIDING REMOVED BY 1929

STATION 63.22

TOU JULY 1936

No 2 GF TOU MAY 1964

ASSOCIATED BRICK AND TILE CO TOU MAY 1964

TOU MAY 1964

To HAVANT

## Idsworth Crossing

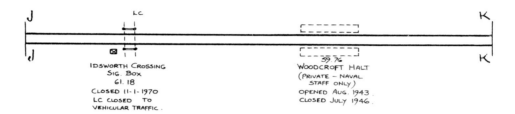

## Buriton Sidings (1906)

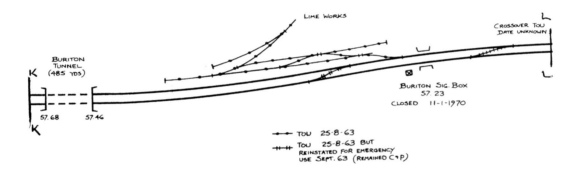

# Petersfield (1903 – August 1969)

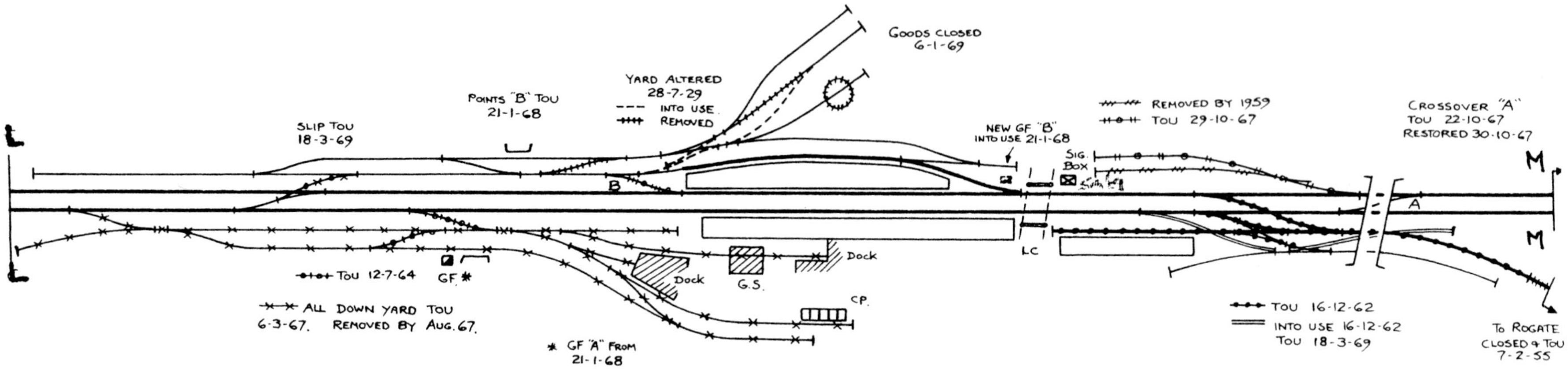

Crossover "A"
Tou 22-10-67
Restored 30-10-67

To Rogate
Closed & Tou
7-2-55

Removed by 1959
Tou 29-10-67

Tou 16-12-62
Into use 16-12-62
Tou 18-3-69

Sig Box

New GF "B"
Into use 21-1-68

Goods closed
6-1-69

LC

Dock

Dock

G.S.

C.P.

Yard altered
28-7-29
Into use
Removed

Points "B" Tou
21-1-68

GF "A" from
21-1-68

Slip Tou
18-3-69

B

Tou 12-7-64

GF *

All down yard Tou
6-3-67. Removed by Aug. 67.

# Liss (1920)

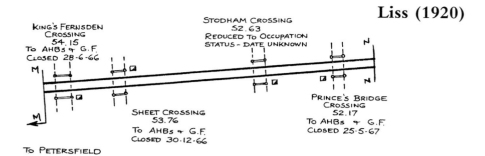

KING'S FERNSDEN
CROSSING
54.15
To AHBs & G.F.
CLOSED 28-6-66

STODHAM CROSSING
52.63
REDUCED TO OCCUPATION
STATUS — DATE UNKNOWN

SHEET CROSSING
53.76
To AHBs & G.F.
CLOSED 30.12.66

PRINCE'S BRIDGE
CROSSING
52.17
To AHBs & G.F.
CLOSED 25.5.67

TO PETERSFIELD

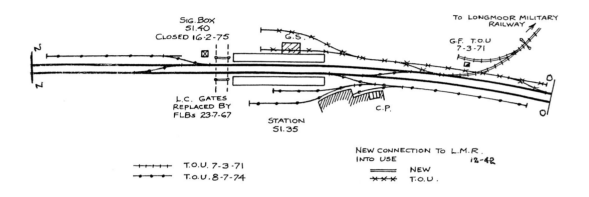

SIG. BOX
51.40
CLOSED 16.2.75

G.S.

To LONGMOOR MILITARY
RAILWAY

G.F. T.O.U
7-3-71

L.C. GATES
REPLACED BY
FLBs 23.7.67

C.P.

STATION
51.35

| | |
|---|---|
| ┼┼┼┼┼┼ | T.O.U. 7-3-71 |
| •┼•┼•┼• | T.O.U. 8-7-74 |

NEW CONNECTION TO L.M.R.
INTO USE          12-42

══════  NEW
××××  T.O.U.

# Liphook (1920)

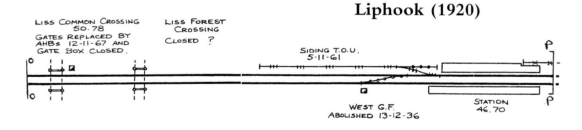

LISS COMMON CROSSING
50.78
GATES REPLACED BY
AHBs 12-11-67 AND
GATE BOX CLOSED.

LISS FOREST
CROSSING
CLOSED ?

SIDING T.O.U.
5-11-61

WEST G.F.
ABOLISHED 13-12-36

STATION
46.70

•┼•┼•┼• REMOVED 13-12-36

EAST G.F.
"LIPHOOK GF" FROM
13-12-36
"G.F. A" FROM 18-6-44
T.O.U. 13-5-69

G.F. "B".
INTO USE 18-6-44
T.O.U. 13-5-69

G.S.

SIG. BOX
CLOSED 16-2-75

SIDING EXTENDED WITH
NEW CONNECTIONS 18-6-44.

| | |
|---|---|
| ×┼×┼×┼× | SIDINGS T.O.U. 13-5-69 |
| ┼○┼○┼ | CROSSOVER T.O.U. 22-7-69 |

- - - -  NEW
┼┼┼┼┼  REMOVED

# Haslemere

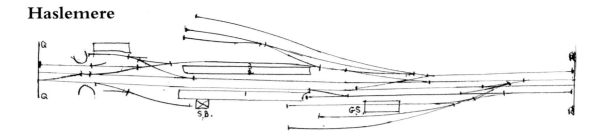

# Witley

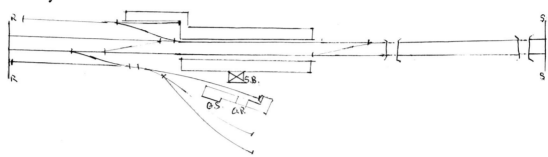

# Milford

# Busbridge Siding

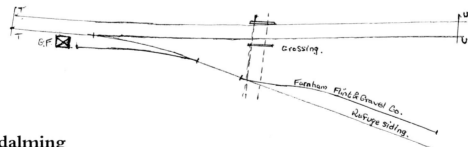

# Godalming

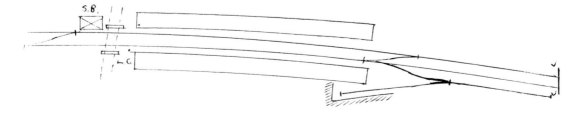

# Godalming

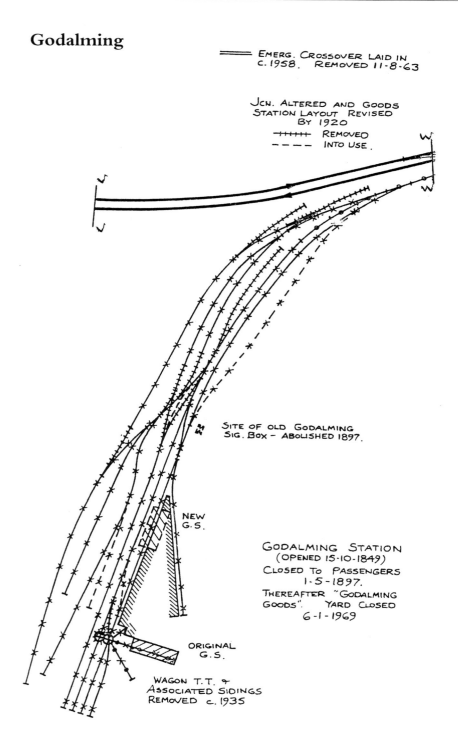

EMERG. CROSSOVER LAID IN
c.1958. REMOVED 11-8-63

JCN. ALTERED AND GOODS
STATION LAYOUT REVISED
BY 1920
++++++ REMOVED
- - - - INTO USE.

SITE OF OLD GODALMING
SIG. BOX – ABOLISHED 1897.

NEW
G.S.

GODALMING STATION
(OPENED 15-10-1849)
CLOSED TO PASSENGERS
1-5-1897.
THEREAFTER "GODALMING
GOODS". YARD CLOSED
6-1-1969

ORIGINAL
G.S.

WAGON T.T. &
ASSOCIATED SIDINGS
REMOVED c.1935

# Farncombe (1897)

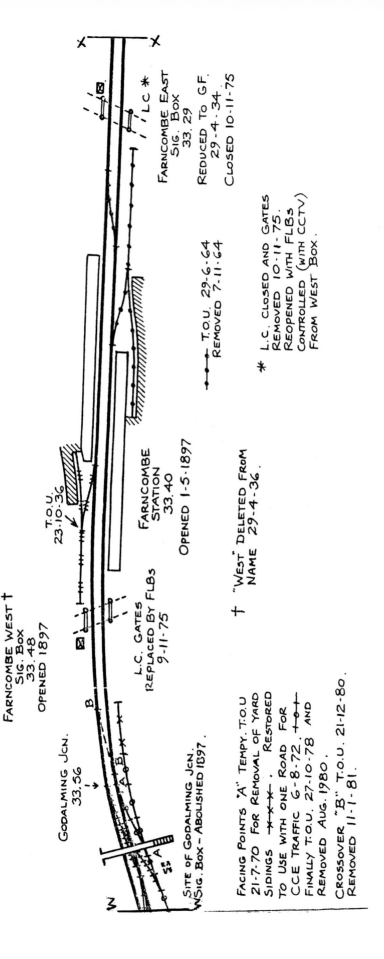

FARNCOMBE WEST † SIG. BOX 33.48 OPENED 1897

GODALMING JCN. 33.56

SITE OF GODALMING JCN. W. SIG. BOX — ABOLISHED 1897.

L.C. GATES REPLACED BY FLBs 9·11·75

FARNCOMBE STATION 33.40 OPENED 1·5·1897

T.O.U. 23·10·36

FARNCOMBE EAST SIG. BOX 33.29 REDUCED TO GF 29·4·34 CLOSED 10·11·75

LC ✱

─•─•─• T.O.U. 29·6·64 REMOVED 7·11·64

✱ L.C. CLOSED AND GATES REMOVED 10·11·75. REOPENED WITH FLBs CONTROLLED (WITH CCTV) FROM WEST BOX.

† "WEST" DELETED FROM NAME 29·4·36.

FACING POINTS "A" TEMPY. T.O.U 21·7·70 FOR REMOVAL OF YARD SIDINGS ─x─x─x─. RESTORED TO USE WITH ONE ROAD FOR CCE TRAFFIC 6·8·72. ─•─ FINALLY T.O.U. 27·10·78 AND REMOVED AUG. 1980.

CROSSOVER "B" T.O.U. 21·12·80. REMOVED 11·1·81.

## Peasmarsh Junction (1920)

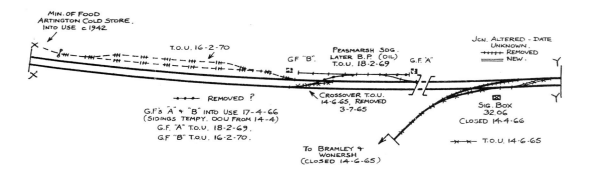

## Shalford Junction (1900)

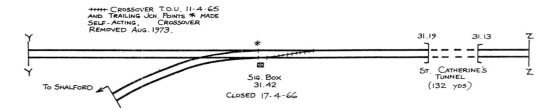

# Guildford (1917)

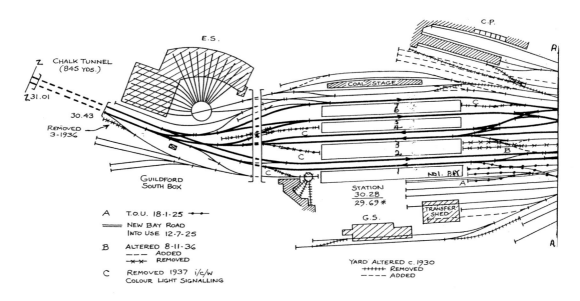

Z CHALK TUNNEL
(845 YDS.)

Z 31.01

E.S.

C.P.

COAL STAGE

30.43

REMOVED
3-1936

GUILDFORD
SOUTH BOX

STATION
30.28
29.69 ✱

G.S.

TRANSFER
SHED

NO.I. BAY

A   T.O.U. 18-1-25 ••—••
    NEW BAY ROAD
    INTO USE 12-7-25

B   ALTERED 8-11-36
    - - - ADDED
    -××- REMOVED

C   REMOVED 1937 i/c/w
    COLOUR LIGHT SIGNALLING

YARD ALTERED c.1930
+++++ REMOVED
- - - - ADDED

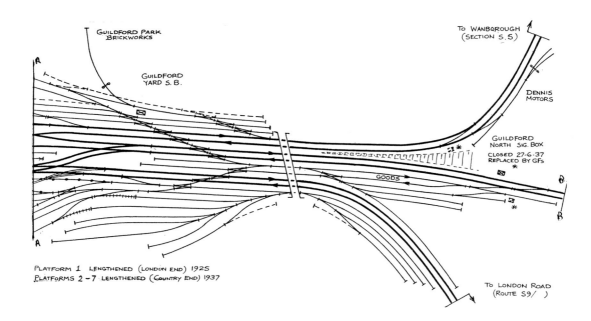

GUILDFORD PARK
BRICKWORKS

TO WANBOROUGH
(SECTION S.5)

GUILDFORD
YARD S.B.

DENNIS
MOTORS

GUILDFORD
NORTH SIG. BOX

CLOSED 27-6-37
REPLACED BY GFS
✱

GOODS

TO LONDON ROAD
(ROUTE S9/ )

PLATFORM 1 LENGTHENED (LONDON END) 1925
PLATFORMS 2-7 LENGTHENED (COUNTRY END) 1937

# Worplesdon (1900)

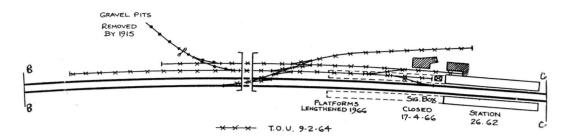

GRAVEL PITS
REMOVED
BY 1915

B

B

PLATFORMS
LENGTHENED 1966

SIG. BOX
CLOSED
17-4-66

STATION
26.62

C

C

—x—x—x—  T.O.U. 9-2-64

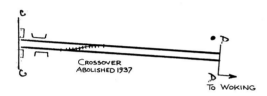

C

C

CROSSOVER
ABOLISHED 1937

D

D
To WOKING

# Woking (1916)

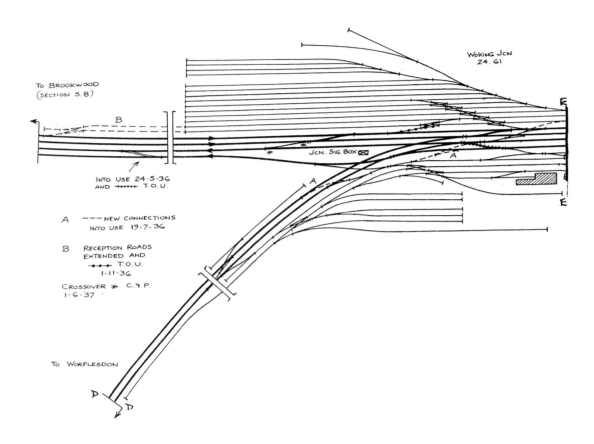

To Brookwood
(Section 5.8)

B

Into use 24.5.36
and ┼┼┼┼ T.O.U.

A ――― New connections
Into use 19-7-36

B Reception Roads
Extended and
┼●┼● T.O.U.
1-11-36

Crossover ✳ C.9 P.
1-6-37

To Worplesdon

Woking Jcn
24.61

Jcn. Sig. Box ⊠

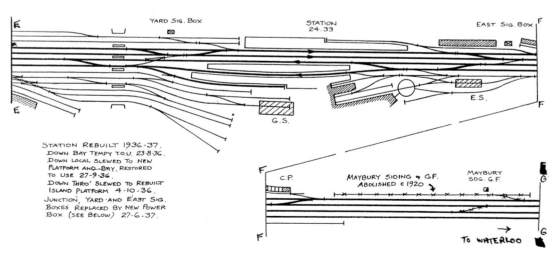

Station Rebuilt 1936-37.
Down Bay Tempy T.O.U. 23-8-36.
Down Local Slewed to new
Platform and Bay, Restored
to use 27-9-36.
Down Thro' Slewed to Rebuilt
Island Platform 4-10-36.
Junction, Yard and East Sig.
Boxes Replaced by New Power
Box (see below) 27-6-37.

Yard Sig. Box
Station
24.33
East Sig. Box

G.S.
E.S.

C.P.
Maybury Siding & G.F.
Abolished c 1920
Maybury
Sdg. G.F.

To Waterloo

# GRADIENT PROFILE

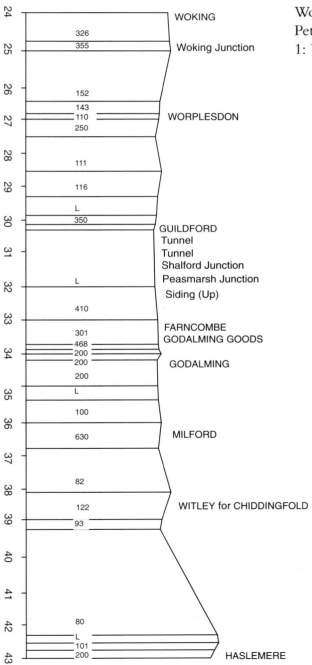

Woking–Guildford–Haslemere–
Petersfield–Portsmouth Harbour
1: Woking to Haslemere

WOKING

326
355  Woking Junction

152
143
110  WORPLESDON
250

111

116

L
350

GUILDFORD
Tunnel
Tunnel
Shalford Junction
Peasmarsh Junction
L
Siding (Up)

410

301  FARNCOMBE
468  GODALMING GOODS
200
200  GODALMING
200

L

100

630  MILFORD

82

122  WITLEY for CHIDDINGFOLD
93

80
L
101
200  HASLEMERE

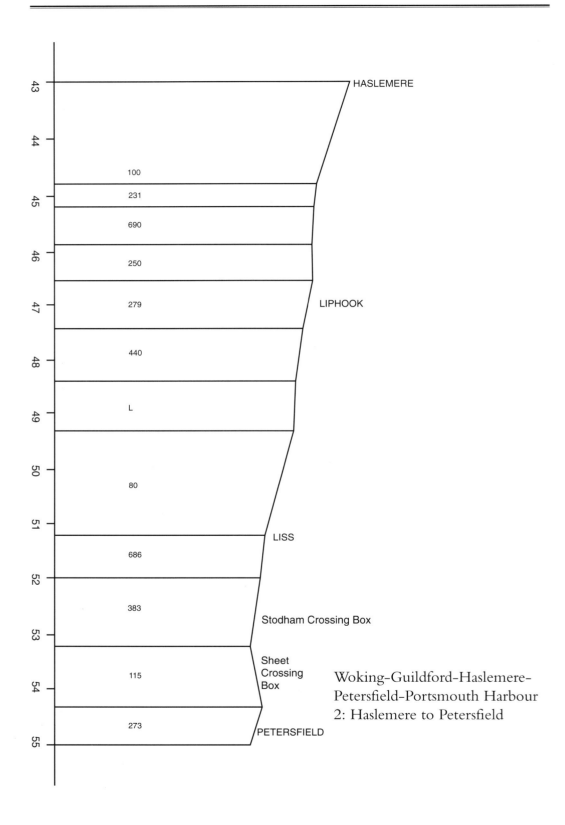

43

44

100

231
45

690

250
46

279
47
LIPHOOK

440
48

L
49

80
50

51
LISS

686
52

383
Stodham Crossing Box

53

Sheet
Crossing
Box
115
54

273
55
PETERSFIELD

HASLEMERE

Woking-Guildford-Haslemere-
Petersfield-Portsmouth Harbour
2: Haslemere to Petersfield

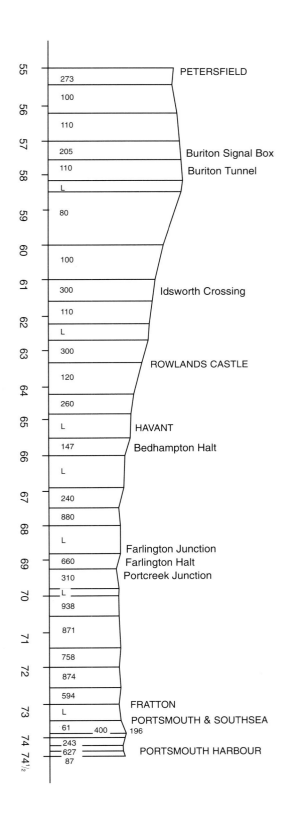

Woking-Guildford-Haslemere-Petersfield-Portsmouth Harbour
3: Petersfield to Portsmouth Harbour

PETERSFIELD
273
100
110
205 — Buriton Signal Box
110 — Buriton Tunnel
L
80
100
300 — Idsworth Crossing
110
L
300
120 — ROWLANDS CASTLE
260
L — HAVANT
147 — Bedhampton Halt
L
240
880
L — Farlington Junction
660 — Farlington Halt
310 — Portcreek Junction
L
938
871
758
874
594 — FRATTON
L — PORTSMOUTH & SOUTHSEA
61   400   196
243
627 — PORTSMOUTH HARBOUR
87

*Appendix III*

# ROUTE MAP

Woking–Guildford–Haslemere–
Petersfield–Portsmouth Harbour
1: Woking to Liphook
(not to scale)

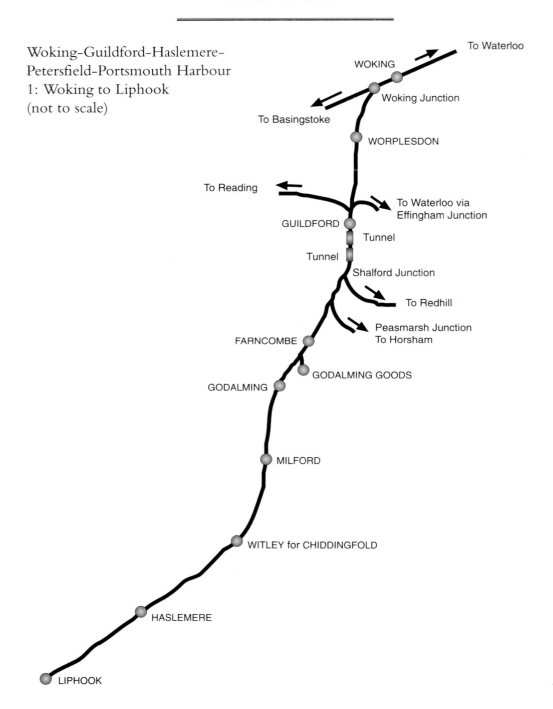

Woking–Guildford–Haslemere–
Petersfield–Portsmouth Harbour
2: Liphook to Portsmouth
Harbour (not to scale)

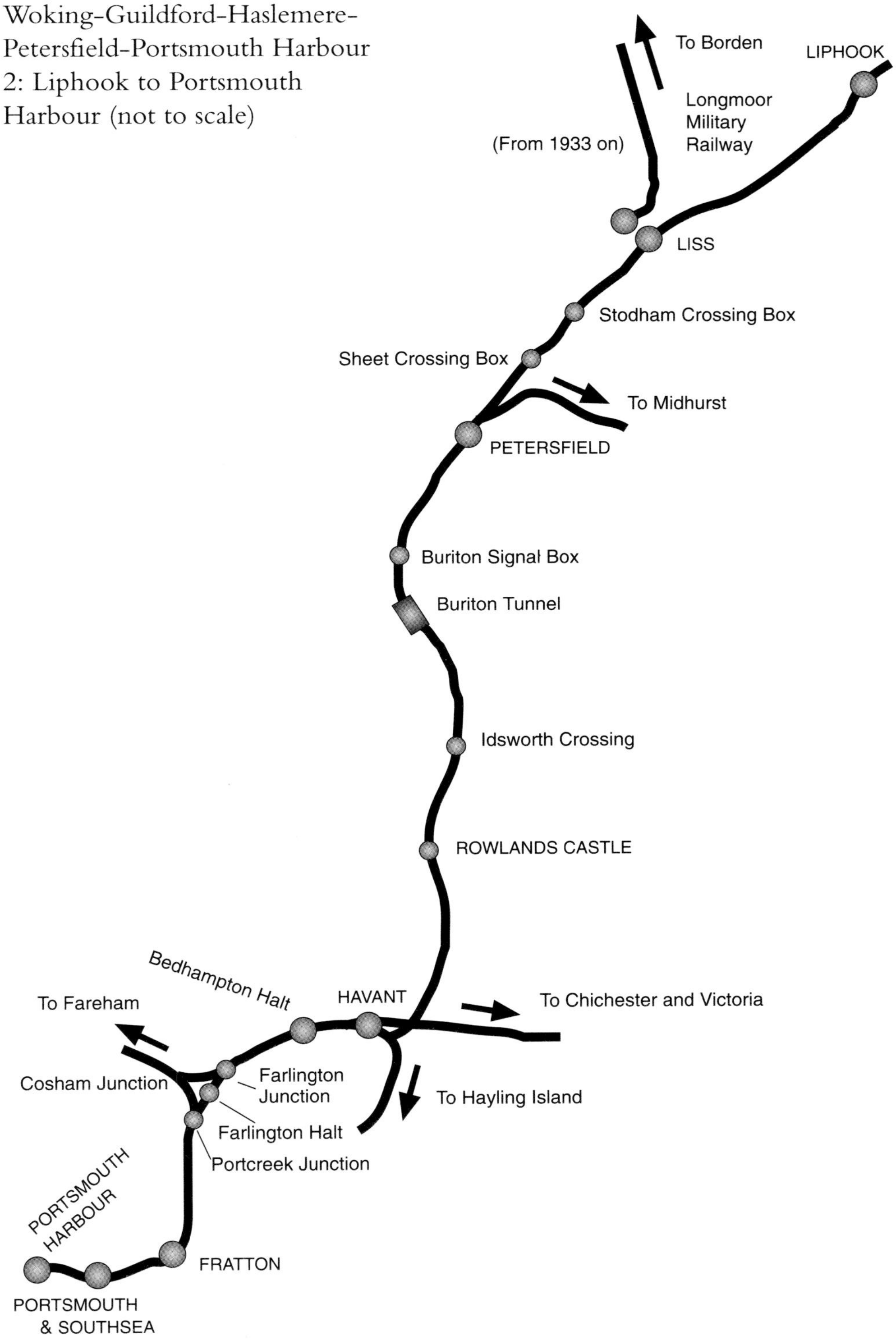

To Borden

LIPHOOK

Longmoor
Military
Railway

(From 1933 on)

LISS

Stodham Crossing Box

Sheet Crossing Box

To Midhurst

PETERSFIELD

Buriton Signal Box

Buriton Tunnel

Idsworth Crossing

ROWLANDS CASTLE

Bedhampton Halt

HAVANT

To Fareham

To Chichester and Victoria

Cosham Junction

Farlington
Junction

To Hayling Island

Farlington Halt

Portcreek Junction

PORTSMOUTH
HARBOUR

FRATTON

PORTSMOUTH
& SOUTHSEA

# LIST OF LOCOMOTIVES

| Class | Type | Cylinders Number/Size (in) | Driving Wheels Diameter | Boiler Pressure (lb/sq in) | SR (Western) Power/Braking group | Capacities Coal/Water (tons/gallons) | Tractive Effort (lb) |
|---|---|---|---|---|---|---|---|
| LN | 4–6–0 | 4/16½ × 26 | 6 ft 7 in | 220 | A | 5/5,000 | 33,510 |
| N15 | 4–6–0 | 2/20½ × 28 | 6 ft 7 in | 200 | A | 5/5,000 | 26,245 |
| H15 | 4–6–0 | 2/21 × 28 | 6 ft 0 in | 180 | A | 5/5,000 | 26,240 |
| S15 | 4–6–0 | 2/20½ × 28 | 5 ft 7 in | 180 | A | 5/5,000 | 28,200 |
| T14 | 4–6–0 | 4/15 × 26 | 6 ft 7 in | 175 | B | 5/5,800 | 22,030 |
| V | 4–4–0 | 3/16½ × 26 | 6 ft 7 in | 220 | A | 5/4,000 | 25,135 |
| D15 | 4–4–0 | 2/20 × 26 | 6 ft 7 in | 180 | D | 5/3,500 | 20,142 |
| T9 | 4–4–0 | 2/19 × 26 | 6 ft 7 in | 175 | H | 5/4,000 | 17,673 |
| X2 | 4–4–0 | 2/19 × 26 | 7 ft 1 in | 175 | I | 5/3,300 | 12,906 |
| K10 | 4–4–0 | 2/19 × 26 | 5 ft 7 in | 175 | F | 5/4,000 | 20,838 |
| L11 | 4–4–0 | 2/19 × 26 | 5 ft 7 in | 175 | F | 5/4,000 | 20,838 |
| L12 | 4–4–0 | 2/19 × 26 | 6 ft 7 in | 175 | D | 5/3,500 | 17,673 |
| 700 | 0–6–0 | 2/19 × 26 | 5 ft 1 in | 180 | C | 4/3,500 | 23,500 |
| 0395 | 0–6–0 | 2/17¾ × 26 | 5 ft 1 in | 140 | G | 4/2,500 | 15,535 |
| 496 | 0–6–0 | 2/17¾ × 26 | 5 ft 1 in | 140 | G | 4/2,500 | 15,535 |
| O2 | 0–4–4T | 2/17½ × 24 | 4 ft 10 in | 160 | K | 1½/800 | 17,245 |
| M7 | 0–4–4T | 2/18½ × 26 | 5 ft 7 in | 175 | K | 3/1,300 | 19,755 |
| G6 | 0–6–0T | 2/17½ × 24 | 4 ft 10 in | 160 | K | 1½/1,000 | 17,245 |
| A12 | 0–4–2 | 2/18 × 26 | 6 ft 1 in | 160 | J | 4/2,350 | 12,502 |
| 0458 | 0–4–0ST | 2/12 × 20 | 3 ft 2 in | 120 | – | | 7,731 |
| H16 | 4–6–2T | 2/21 × 28 | 5 ft 7 in | 180 | A | 3½/2,000 | 28,200 |
| U | 2–6–0 | 2/19 × 28 | 6 ft 0 in | 200 | – | 5/4,000 | 23,866 |
| U1 | 2–6–0 | 3/16 × 28 | 6 ft 0 in | 200 | – | 5/4,000 | 25,387 |
| N | 2–6–0 | 2/19 × 28 | 5 ft 6 in | 200 | – | 5/4,000 | 26,035 |
| N1 | 2–6–0 | 3/16 × 28 | 5 ft 6 in | 200 | – | 5/4,000 | 27,695 |
| D1 | 4–4–0 | 2/19 × 26 | 6 ft 8 in | 180 | – | 4½/3,300 | 17,950 |
| E1 | 4–4–0 | 2/19 × 26 | 6 ft 6 in | 180 | – | 4½/3,300 | 18,410 |
| F1 | 4–4–0 | 2/18 × 26 | 7 ft 0 in | 170 | – | 2,650 | 14,491 |
| K1 | 2–6–4T | 3/16 × 28 | 6 ft 0 in | 200 | – | 2½/2,000 | 25,387 |
| K | 2–6–4T | 2/19 × 28 | 6 ft 0 in | 200 | – | 2½/2,000 | 23,866 |
| K | 2–6–0 | 2/21 × 26 | 5 ft 6 in | 170 | – | 4/3,940 | 25,100 |
| C2X | 0–6–0 | 2/17½ × 26 | 5 ft 0 in | 170 | – | | 19,175 |
| D1 | 0–4–2T | 2/17 × 24 | 5 ft 6 in | 140 | – | | 12,506 |
| A1X | 0–6–0T | 2/12 × 20 | 4 ft 0 in | 150 | – | 1/500 | 7,648 |
| E1 | 0–6–0T | 2/17 × 24 | 4 ft 6 in | 160 | – | 1½/900 | 17,500 |
| E3 | 0–6–2T | 2/17½ × 26 | 4 ft 6 in | 170 | – | 2½/1,377 | 21,307 |
| E4 | 0–6–2T | 2/17½ × 26 | 5 ft 0 in | 170 | – | | 19,175 |
| B4X | 4–4–0 | 2/20 × 26 | 6 ft 9 in | 180 | – | | 19,644 |
| H2 | 4–4–2 | 2/21 × 26 | 6 ft 7½ in | 200 | – | 4/3,500 | 24,520 |

*Notes*  1.  Ex-LBSCR engines ran over the Havant to Portsmouth Harbour section during normal working. A1X engines also worked the branch from Havant to Hayling Island.

      2.  Ex-LBSCR 4–4–2 Atlantic No. B425 *Trevose Head* is recorded as having worked a Waterloo to Portsmouth Harbour train on at least one occasion.

      3.  Where locomotive details cannot be confirmed, the column has been left blank.

# BIBLIOGRAPHY

Bell, R. OBE. 'History of the British Railways during the war 1939–1945', *Railway Gazette*, 1946

Bonavia, M.R. MA, PhD, FCIT. *The History of the Southern Railway*, Unwin Hyman, 1987

Bradley, D.L. *London & South Western Railway Steam Album*, Ian Allan, 1976

Casserley, H.C. *Railway Locomotives of Britain*, Frederick Warne, 1957

Course, Edwin. BSc (Econ), PhD, AMIInstT. *Portsmouth Railways*, Portsmouth, Portsmouth City Library, 1969

Darwen, B. *War on the Line*, Southern Railway, 1946

Hamilton Ellis, C. AILocoE, FRSA. *The South Western Railway*, Allen & Unwin, 1956

Nock, O.S. BSc, CEng, MICE, MIMechE, MILocoE. *North Western*, Ian Allan, 1968

—— *Southern Steam*, Newton Abbot, David & Charles, 1966

Pryer, G.A., and Paul, A.V. *Track Layout Diagrams of the Southern Railway*, Harwell, Cooke, 1981

*Railway Magazine*

Ransome Wallis, P. *The Last Steam Locomotives of British Railways*, Leicester, Magna Books, 1993

Ronald, D.W., and Carter, R.J. *The Longmoor Military Railway*, Newton Abbot, David & Charles, 1974

# INDEX